ANCIENT EGYPTIAN MYTHOLOGY

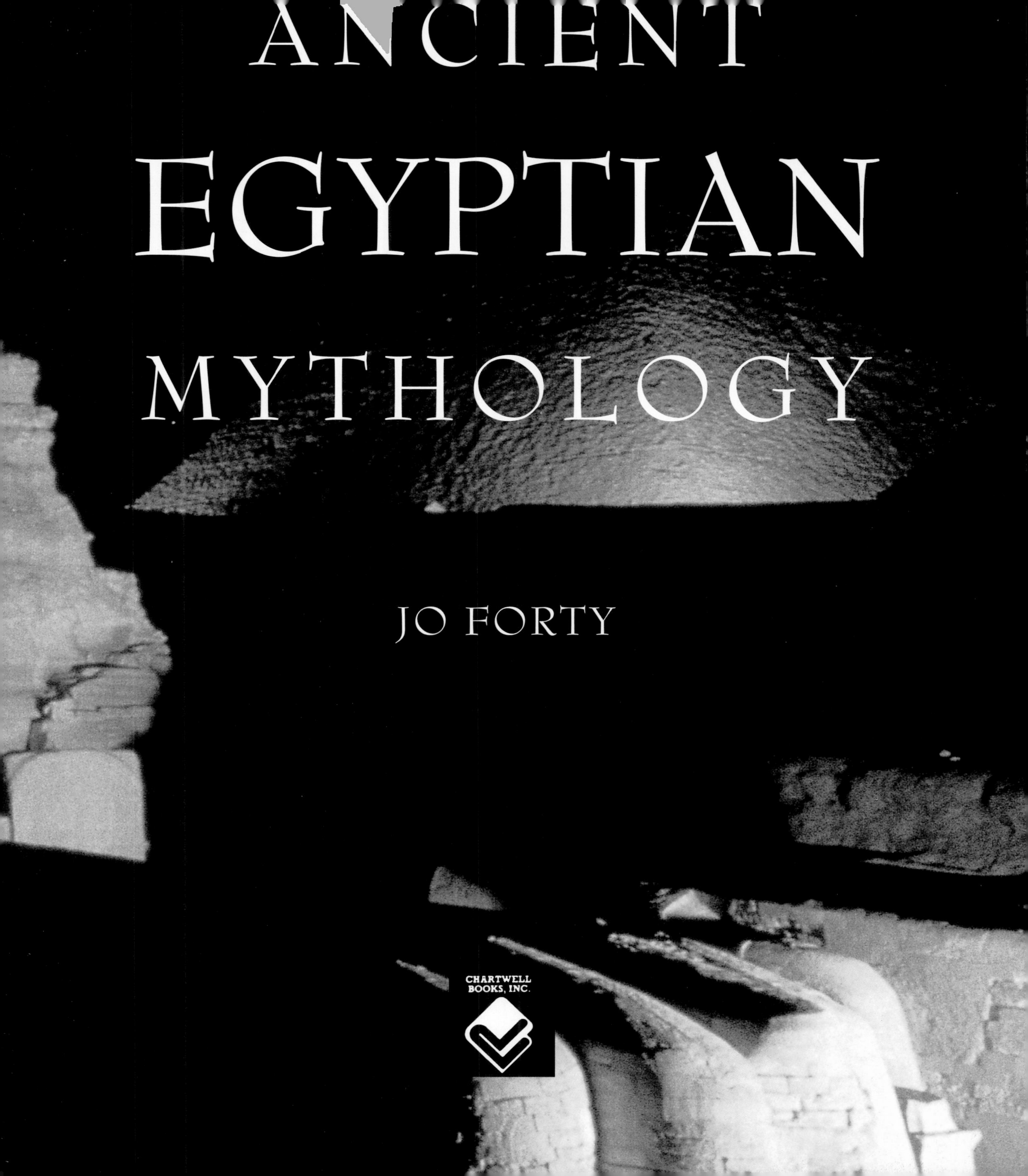

ANCIENT EGYPTIAN MYTHOLOGY

JO FORTY

CHARTWELL BOOKS, INC.

This edition first published in 1996 by the
Promotional Reprint Company Ltd,
Kiln House,
210 New Kings Road,
London SW6 4NZ.

CHARTWELL BOOKS. INC.
A division of BOOK SALES, INC
P.O. Box 7100
Edison, New Jersey 08818-7100

ISBN 07858 07667

Printed and bound in China

Acknowledgements
The Publisher and Author gratefully acknowledge the provision of photographs for this book seen by Christie's Images (as credited) and the Egyptian Tourist Board

HALF TITLE PAGE:

The temple of Harwer — Horus the Elder — and the crocodile-headed Sobek at Kom Ombo, from the Ptolemaic period. The temple is symmetrical about a central axis, the eastern half belonging to Sobek, the western to Harwer.

TITLE PAGE:

The classic view of Ancient Egypt: son et lumière of the Great Sphinx and, behind it, the pyramids of Khafre (left) and Khufu at Giza.

CONTENTS PAGE:

Avenue of rams at Karnak.

CONTENTS

The Ancient Egyptians

THE White Nile originates deep in Equatorial Africa; the Blue Nile high in the Ethiopian Mountains. They converge on present day Khartoum and together they combine to form one of the world's longest and most regular rivers, from whose desert oases and fan-shaped delta sprang an astonishing 4,000-year old civilisation. Agriculturally based, this early civilisation was to leave behind the amazing technological achievements of its temples, tombs and, its most lasting landmarks, the Pyramids. Its people's imagination and zest for life wove as complex a web of belief and ritual, cultural explanation and rationale, as could be found anywhere at any time.

The Ancient Egyptians and their gods functioned for a period of time approximately twice as long as our current Christian era. With the desert making natural geographical frontiers, the Nile dwellers had the safety of isolation in which to develop their completely unique approach to life. Beginning in pre-dynastic times Neolithic hunter-gatherers settled along the river's edge as the Sahara dried out, gradually co-operating more and more in the management of the annual inundation that occurred with dependable regularity, bringing with it a rich black alluvial silt to fertilise their fields. This silt gave the name to their country — 'Khemet', the Black Land — and it was surrounded by the aridity of the Red Land — 'Dehsret'. From independent beginnings they organised themselves, firstly into villages, next to federations of communities, then small provinces, the later 'nomes'.

By about 3500 BC two large kingdoms had emerged — the Two Lands: Upper Egypt, from the first cataract of the Nile at Elephantine almost to the edge of the delta; and Lower Egypt, the delta area itself. Upper Egypt was known as the

BELOW: Pyramids at Giza: in the foreground the three smaller pyramids of Menkaure's queens, and behind them that of Menkaure himself. In the centre, the Pyramid of Khafre, with a considerable part of its outer casing still in place at its apex. This pyramid seems the largest of the clump, because it was built on higher ground, but it is the last pyramid in line, the Great Pyramid of Khufu, that is the earliest, the largest and the most important of the whole group. Its fantastic size (over 2.3 million stone blocks averaging 2.5 tons each) and the perfection of its constuction make it one of the foremost architectural achievements of mankind.

White Land, with its capital city at Nehken (Hieraconpolis), near Edfu. The kingdom's deities were the hawk-headed Horus, and vulture goddess Nehkbet, and the king wore the tall White crown. Lower Egypt was called the Red Land, with its capital city at Pe, also called Buto. Here the king wore the Red crown, and the cobra-goddess Edjo was worshipped, along with the composite animal god Set. These two kingdoms were finally united around 3100 BC, but their origins were never forgotten, instead the duality was celebrated in the title 'The Two Lands' and the new Double crown combined both the red and the white crowns, with the two protective goddesses included.

Because of its location on the Mediterranean, the Nile delta was the meeting point for trade, immigration and technology from the continents of Asia, Africa and Europe; whilst the south, with considerably less contact with the outside world, retained its traditions and culture much more deeply.

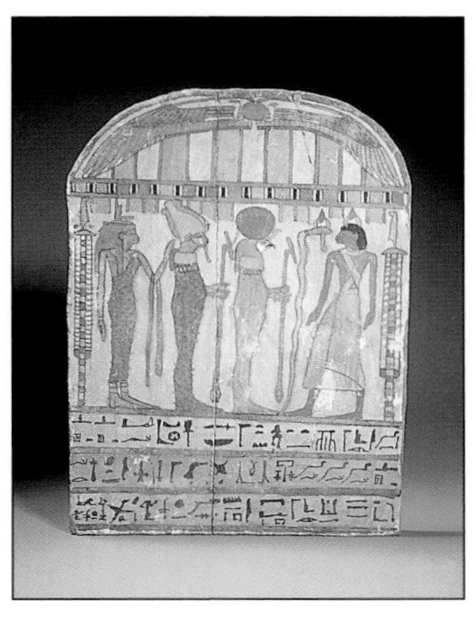

ABOVE: Gesso-painted wooden stele. At right a deceased man being presented by hawk-headed Horus to Osiris. Behind Osiris stands Isis. Stelae were usually made of stone or wood; funerary stelae were left in tombs to ensure a happy and comfortable time in the Underworld for the newly departed. They would inform the gods of the importance of the deceased with his portrait, his name, status and titles, plus all the goods and chattels he was bringing with him such as food, drink and luxuries. There were also votive stelae praising the gods and asking for beneficence; these were usually placed in temples. Christie's Images

The Two Lands were united by Narmer, also known as Menes. Thus Horus of Behdet, the national god of Upper Egypt, triumphed over Set of Ombus, his rival in the Delta, and became the state god of the Two Lands. Narmer established a new capital at Memphis and inaugurated the first dynasty (3050-2890 BC) of ancient Egyptian history. This period saw the evolution of the Pharaoh as absolute ruler, a god himself in his capacity as head of state, and the earthly embodiment of Horus. There was a homogeneity of culture yet without the centralisation of the later Old Kingdom. The gods of the more influential cities similarly acquired national status as the Two Lands fused.

From the outset Egyptians were intensely religious and superstitious; the supernatural was closely interwoven with the real in many aspects of everyday life. Furthermore, as the state deities became incorporated into the government structure, so the primarily agricultural population coped with the everyday hazards of life by recourse to magic, spells, charms and folklore; they appealed to the zooamorphic gods of each hazard to intercede on their behalf — such as the Nile, sowing, harvest, scorpions and snakes, childbirth, etc — and the local gods with the character of their locality. These, by their very nature, leave little trace for us to analyse, and for the most part, archaeological evidence is more concerned with the monumental remains left to history.

As the villages grew into towns, and then to cities, their gods grew in stature likewise. Through synthesis and syncretism, the growth of the pantheon reflects the growth of the country. Other features of these early dynasties were the development of building in stone, and the obsession with the correct procedure for attaining life after death, both of which were destined to become lasting cultural habits. The kings of these proto-dynasties built mastaba — stepped — tombs at Neqada, Abydos, Saqqara and Helouam, including the legendary Imhotep's step pyramid — the earliest stone building of its size in the world.

2575 BC ushered in the 4th Dynasty, and the golden age of the pyramids of the Old Kingdom. There were major advances in the fields of art and architecture; and trading expeditions to Nubia.

During this time, it was believed that only the pharaoh received everlasting life; everyone else could take part through their contribution of service to the pharaoh, both while he was alive in this world and when he went on to eternity. So the construction of the royal pyramid complex became the focus of the whole society, of vital importance to everyone — the pharaoh and his subjects — and huge resources were used to achieve this aim.

Also at this time there was an attempt to rationalise the incredible number of gods and the wide variety of religious beliefs, into a more cohesive whole. As the larger cities became great religious centres, so various deities merged or became

ABOVE: A stone recumbent sphinx. In Ancient Egypt the image of the sphinx was a powerful religious and royal symbol of power and authority. However the image was adopted and adapted largely as an ornament by other cultures — for example as here, the ancient Greek sphinx had a lion's body with a female head and breasts, the whole representing enigmatic wisdom. Christie's Images

RIGHT: Red quartzite head of Akhenaten. Regarded as the heretic pharaoh for overthrowing all other gods and goddesses in the pantheon in favour of the exclusive monotheistic worship of Aten, till then a relatively obscure manifestation of the sun deity. Whether it was chiefly for religious or political ends is uncertain, but Akhenaten's reign ushered in other changes in the arts of sculpture, painting and literature, which are known today as the Amarna style, after the area in which his obliterated capital was built. Christie's Images

linked in groups or 'families', each with its own distinctive, yet similar, creation myth. The largest cities at the time were Memphis, Heliopolis and Hermopolis.

By the 6th Dynasty the Old Kingdom was beginning to succumb to its own limitations; there was too great a centralisation of power, too much tax pressure on farmers, and too many resources were being used in the building and maintenance of the huge pharaonic funerary complexes. The priesthoods and local governors had become very wealthy and powerful at the expense of the pharaoh, and gradually the country broke back down into its provincial beginnings.

The First Intermediate period saw the Two Lands splintered, with foreigners entering the Nile delta, alongside a rapid change and high turnover of Pharaohs. During this time of upheaval, religious beliefs and customs inevitably underwent dramatic changes too. With the idea of the god-king discredited, people now wanted their own personal eternity, and as a consequence Osiris rose to prominence to fulfil this desire.

There was a minor Hierakliopolitan resurgence in the 9th and 10th Dynasties, but they were overwhelmed by a new Theban line, who reunited the country, leading to the Middle Kingdom period. Montu, the Theban god of war, became dominant, before giving way to Amun in the 12th Dynasty. This was a period of expansion, immigration and trade. There were campaigns in Nubia to keep the vital gold routes open, and a lot more contact with outsiders coming into the delta; expeditions were made to Punt and into Sinai. The country was reorganised and land reclamation schemes pursued, the highlight of which was the reopening of the ancient irrigation system, repaired to its former glory.

The pharaohs of this 12th Dynasty tried to reduce the power of the local nobility, to establish the dominance of Thebes; but while Amun was the main pharaonic god, they supported other cults too: Ptah at Memphis, Hathor at Dendera, Min at Coptos, Re'-Atum at Heliopolis, Sobek in the Faiyum and Osiris at Abydos. There was also increased democratisation of the Afterlife — a result of the universal appeal of Osiris.

At death, regardless of personal wealth or position, one was judged in the presence of Osiris by 42 Assessor Gods, and one's heart went in the scales weighted opposite Ma'at's feather of truth and justice. Passing this test guaranteed eternal life with Osiris, and there was consequently a much wider distribution of non-royal tombs and an increased range of funerary equipment.

The Second Intermediate period came about again through weak rulers and simultaneous dynasties competing from their different bases at Thebes and in the delta at Xois. This internal confusion enabled Middle Eastern outsiders, the Hyksos, to come pouring in to the delta and, for a time, take over almost the whole country. Their leaders became pharaohs, and they adopted local gods and traditions (with the unfortunate choice of Set as their main royal god). The Hyksos brought with them various technological innovations — in arms, construction, metallurgy and agriculture, but relations between them and the indigenous population soured.

There was another resurgence at Thebes, in the 17th Dynasty, which finally managed to expel the foreigners, and set the stage for the final great flowering of ancient Egyptian civilisation: the New Kingdom 1570-1085 BC. Now Egypt was no longer isolated, but an important part of the ancient Mediterranean world. There was a need for trade and just as important, to establish borders and zones of Egyptian control and influence.

The pharaohs of the 18th Dynasty by these means expanded their country and built an empire — conquering Palestine, reaching as far as the Euphrates in Syria, securing the delta to both east and west with fortifications, penetrating south as far

as the 4th cataract of the Nile, and securing control of the Nubian gold mines. Egypt was asserting itself in the face of increasing competition from Libyans, Hittites, sea people, Nubians and all the other tribes and groups pushing each other onwards in the restless development and exchange of early civilisation.

Soon other greater waves would overwhelm them too, but for now Egypt had an empire, with 2,000 years of history and experience already behind her, and was the wealthiest country in the world, with tribute pouring in from all corners. The capital was at Thebes, and the air-god Amun was combined with the creator sun-god Re' into the supreme state god Amun-Re'. His magnificent temple complex at Karnak became the most powerful religious and political centre in the empire. Eventually, through this power, the priesthood would come to wield such influence as to control the royal line of succession and turn Egypt into an ecclesiastical state. The tombs of the pharaohs were hidden in a valley (the Valley of the Kings), cut into rock, as they eschewed the pyramids that were so easily robbed and desecrated. Their families and followers were once again buried nearby in their own necropoli.

The 18th and 19th Dynasties saw a fantastic rise in construction all over the country. Some of the most well known pharaohs achieved such status because of the vast wealth at their disposal, and therefore the sheer number of monuments and buildings, temples, forts, tombs and statues bearing their names. In recognition of their successes the pharaohs heaped treasure on Amun-Re', but as his priesthood became increasingly rich and influential, the Pharaohs had cause to regret it, and tried to curtail their power.

One method the pharaohs adopted to circumvent the priesthood was that of co-regency, when an elder pharaoh had his heir already acknowledged and active in his government. Perhaps Akhenaten (originally Amenhotep IV) and his attempt at monotheism with Aten was mainly to break the power of the priesthood of Amun-Re'. If so it failed, for Aten had no popular acceptance, and was too abstract a deity to appeal to the masses; when Akhenaten died, Aten went with him and the old gods were restored.

By the time of the 20th Dynasty a high proportion of land had passed to the temples, and especially that of Amun at Karnak, to the point where it virtually controlled the whole of Upper Egypt. The priesthood became hereditary and independent of the pharaoh, forming its own dynasty that became strong enough to rival the state itself. Within the royal line too there were conspiracies and jostling for position that only served to weaken the whole succession. There were strikes too among the royal workmen; dissatisfaction and unrest spread.

Finally when the throne fell to a high-priest, Lower Egypt defected, and Nubia broke away. The nearer eastern possessions had already been absorbed by the expanding Hittite and Babylonian nations. The 21st Dynasty ruled from Tanis in the Nile delta, with only token acknowledgement from Thebes. Gradually relations between the two improved enough for intermarriage to take place between the royal and hereditary priesthood lines, until the two were united in form if not reality.

The 22nd Dynasty ruled from Bubastis in the delta and was of Libyan extraction, but after an initial increase in prosperity, there was a period of conflict and decline, with numerous simultaneous local dynasties; the 24th at Sais in the Delta, and the 25th, a Nubian line, recognised as far as Thebes. Both the institutions of pharaoh and priesthood were severely weakened at this time; perhaps the priesthood of Amun at Thebes suffered more because the pharaohs were able to 'marry' their daughters to Amun, thus they became a divine wife and therefore unable to marry any mortal. This development manifested the pharaoh's power at Thebes.

RIGHT: The pharoahs of the 18th and 19th Dynasties were proud, rich and powerful — and great builders: none more so than Rameses II 'the Great' who ruled from 1290BC to 1224BC. He extended the Temple of Amun at Luxor which had been started by Amenhotep III. This photograph is taken from the Court of Rameses II and looks past the gigantic figure of the pharaoh (a similar seated figure sits on the other side) through to the magnificent colonnade of Amenhotep III which leads to his court.

After an initially prosperous start the 25th Dynasty came into conflict with the newly-emergent Assyrian power that was expanding eastwards. At first held at bay, the Assyrians finally took Memphis in 671 BC, and drove the pharaoh south, from where he briefly counter-attacked. But by 650 BC the Assyrians were in control, ruling through a noble line from Sais.

Eventually, however, Assyrian domination was cast off by the pharaohs of the 26th Dynasty, which had started in 668 BC during the period of struggle. A new development at this time was the use of Greek mercenaries in military campaigns — a usage that increased over the next three centuries. The city of Naucratis was specifically given by the Egyptian authorities to these Greek mercenaries and their hangers' on with the intention of preventing the intermingling of the foreigners with the native population.

As Assyrian power waned, the Babylonians and Medes filled the vacuum, and Egypt found itself making an alliance with its old enemy and with its erstwhile possessions, the Palestinian states, in an attempt to balance this latest threat. But in 539 BC Babylon itself was overthrown by a newly emergent power: Persia, which conquered Babylon and invaded Egypt. Following the siege and fall of Memphis in around 520 BC, the pharaoh was put to death and Egypt became a satrapy of the Persian empire.

Some Persian kings were more highly motivated than others in their rule over the Two Lands, but by and large the country was ruthlessly exploited with very little being put back in return. Uprisings were pitilessly suppressed, and the Egyptians were forced to tolerate Persian rule as there was simply no other alternative. As soon as one arose there was an immediate appeal for help — so once again Egypt had recourse to Greek military aid, this time from the city-state of Athens. But with the peace treaty between Athens and Persia of 449 BC, there was only a short period of freedom for the 28th, 29th and 30th Dynasties, before the Persians savagely reimposed their rule in 343 BC. They were to remain in power until Alexander the Great swept their empire into history in 332 BC.

Alexander took Egypt without bloodshed and was widely welcomed as a saviour; and, as in all his conquests, he behaved with foresight and compassion. Local traditions and culture were tolerated and religious freedom encouraged. He hoped to bind his vast empire together with common ideals of mutual freedom and respect, and had he lived no doubt his approach would have had far-reaching effects.

In the short time he was in the country, Alexander reorganised the government, mainly in the military and financial departments; he also accorded the gods particular respect, and travelled to Siwah, the distant oracle of Jupiter-Amun, where he received acknowledgement from the god and therefore acceptance from the native population and eventual deification.

With Alexander's death Egypt fell to his most able general — Ptolemy — who founded a dynasty that spanned 250 years, and saw the Hellenisation of much Egyptian culture, though the exchange was by no means all one way. The Ptolemeic pharaohs adopted the Egyptian tradition of royal brother-sister marriage. They restored and built temples in the traditional manner, and created a hybrid Greco-Egyptian god: Serapis, a combination of elements of Osiris, Zeus, Helios and Aesculapius.

Under the Ptolemaic pharaohs the Greeks spread out across the country from the cities of Alexandria and Naucratis; they also colonised the fertile Faiyum, an oasis with a large lake fed by the Bahr Yusef, a branch of the Nile that diverges from the main river to the west.

The abolition of the old Egyptian aristocracy paved the way for the creation of

a new, predominantly Greek, nobility. There was the occasional native uprising, especially in the area of Thebes, but these were always easily suppressed. The only real danger to the Ptolemeic succession came from itself — with constant internal bickering and struggles for succession. Alongside this Hellenisation there was growth in sculpture, and also a huge increase in animal worship — an overlap of Greek and Egyptian religious cultures.

The dynasty ended with the famous Cleopatra, that artful queen who strove vainly to protect her country from Roman dominion. But it was not to be, and with her death Egypt became little more than the granary of the Roman empire — exploited without compunction. Only the occasional emperor showed any personal interest in the country, with only the most token acknowledgement of Egyptian cultural processes. Unlike other provinces of the Roman empire, Egypt was given no autonomy, but was governed directly by the emperor through the prefect.

The Romans followed the example of the Greeks in accepting and adopting the titles of 'Pharaoh and Divine Son', since it gave them the legitimacy to rule, and so to exploit the Two Lands for Rome's benefit. But the native culture continued among true Egyptians until the advent of Christianity. Rome, too, eventually succumbed to Christianity, having fought unsuccessfully to suppress this new religion, and finally in 311 BC Constantine, the first Christian emperor, issued the Edict of Tolerance, effectively converting to Christianity as the state religion.

During Emperor Constantine's reign, Christianity spread throughout Egypt, and the government was reorganised into a diocese of six provinces. There were persecutions of pagans and heretics; the old gods and their temples were attacked and the old faiths were destroyed. However it was not until AD 540, that the last temples, on the island of Philae near Elephantine, were closed, and the old ancient gods of Egypt, after almost 4,000 years, died.

ABOVE: Alexander the Great's bloodless conquest of Egypt was to change the country completely. Welcomed as the man who had rid the country of the Persians, he was crowned in 332BC and stayed in Egypt for six months.

Following Alexander's death in Babylon in 323BC, his general Ptolemy and the dynasty he founded was to rule Egypt from the great new city of Alexandria — planned before Alexander's death — until conquered by the Romans. The Ptolemaic Kingdom was based on trade with the cities of Asia Minor and the Aegean League, which was formed under Egypt's influence. The Greeks restored many of the temples and adopted the worship of the Egyptian gods — albeit with strong Hellenisation: thus Amun became Zeus, Hathor Aphrodite, etc.

Alexander's body was brought to Egypt by Ptolemy — hijacked as it was en route to Macedonia. It is said to have laid in state in Memphis before later burial in Alexandria.

This painting shows Alexander rewarding his captains, after Fernandi Francesco Calle D Imperiali. Christie's Images

Religion in Ancient Egypt

THE Ancient Egyptians lived in an intensely religious society with a polytheism that was both complex and ritualised. Along the length of the Nile innumerable local cults had grown within each settlement, and while each had its own mythology, they were all variants on a common theme, connected to the natural cycles of the sun and the river, life and death.

Gods were more prominent than myths, and whereas some were defined by myth, others were very much local, taking their appearance and personality from a particular aspect in the environment — the sun, the Nile, crop sowing and the harvest, crafts and trades, and animals — both domestic and wild. Reflecting the inherent dualism of the Two Lands many gods merged and combined features, aspects and personality traits.

As the bigger and more influential cities acquired national status, so too did their gods. Creator-god Ptah of Memphis, sun-god Re' of Heliopolis, fertility-god Min of Coptos, Hathor of Dendera, Osiris of Abydos, Neith of Sais and the cosmic god Amun of Hermopolis and later Thebes: these were all localised divinities whose cults became widespread. Similarly, Horus of Behdet and Set of Ombos were originally local gods of provincial capitals who were elevated to national status as chief gods of their respective southern and northern states.

BELOW: A Djed column: symbol of continual stability, it is thought to have originated from the form of papyrus bound in a column. It was often buried with a mummy as a powerful amulet indicating the backbone of Osiris with the horizontal rows representing his crown. Christie's Images

Eventually, following the conquest of Lower Egypt by its upper, southern counterpart, Horus prevailed and ruled triumphant. The pharaoh, a god himself in his capacity as head of state, was believed to be the earthly embodiment of Horus, and was thus an interface between the people and the gods. As a manifestation of the creator-god on Earth, the pharaoh re-enacted through ceremony and ritual the role of making order out of chaos, keeping the ship of state on an even keel. Most pharaohs sought to enhance their status by emphasising this connection and deifying themselves, often before death.

Gods who moved location occasionally superseded the local god; so Montu, the Theban god of war, was overshadowed by Amun, who became king of the gods when he combined with Re' of Heliopolis. Osiris, too, was not native to Abydos, but was the most loved of all the Egyptian Gods.

Gods were also combined into groups or families in an attempt to rationalise the pantheon, as the sheer number must have been confusing to the ancient Egyptians themselves! It is sometimes difficult to distinguish between local gods and divinities of a different order. Cosmic deities were usually anthropomorphic, whereas more local gods tended to be manifested in animal form, and continued to be worshipped and represented as animals, or as humans with animal heads.

The religion had three basic aspects: the first two, the official State and Mortuary spheres, are both well documented, with much archaeological evidence. These aspects took the form of observance of ritual and cult practices carried out by the pharaoh and the various priesthoods in temples that were off-limits to the rest of the population. In the earlier periods these priesthoods were usually related to the pharaoh. Inside, through correct procedure and observance, the gods took up residence in their images, and acknowledged the pharaoh and through him society as a whole. It was only during festivals and special celebrations, although without actually seeing the images, that the public had access to the god and took part in the state-managed parades.

ABOVE: A hierocephalous deity (one whose head is that of a god) — such images were usually only worshipped locally. Most of the gods took on a feared or venerated animal aspect and when worshipped in that image were considered to be the living manifestation of the gods. Christie's Images

At his death, the pharaoh became one with Osiris and lived with Re', and through his pyramid complex could live on with all his needs provided for — incarcerated with him was virtually everything he had in his earthly life copied, painted and represented for the afterlife. The first pharaohs even had their wives and retainers buried with them, but this population-intensive sacrifice was soon substituted with representational figures, carvings and paintings. The preservation of the corpse became increasingly important and evolved into a complicated religious process — all part of equipping the pharaoh (and eventually the nobility) with what was necessary for an eternally happy and luxurious afterlife.

The third aspect was the everyday popular religion of the bulk of the population. Today, unfortunately, the details of this are not nearly so well known as there is very little primary evidence. The gods did not mingle with men, yet were subject to the same emotions — love, hate, jealousy and revenge. There was a strong belief in magic and folklore, and the peasants were very superstitious: with amulets, charms, spells and prayers, they sought to protect themselves from the many dangers, demons and everyday hazards of life. The gods they worshipped were not cosmic but local, and took the form of everyday animals — an ibis, a crocodile, a hippopotamus, a ram, a bull, a baboon, a cat. All have been found buried and dedicated to the gods of whom they were the living manifestations. They were invariably worshipped at small local shrines, built of temporary materials that leave little archaeological trace.

As time moved on the central institution of the monarchy — the pharaoh — lost much of its dynamism, but this did not lead to a lessening of religious belief. On

ABOVE and RIGHT: The rich Theban kings of the 18th Dynasty started to build royal tombs in a valley behind Deir el-Bahri — it would become known as the Valley of the Kings. 62 tombs have been discovered there, although not all of them are royal.

The earliest tomb is that of Thutmose I; the latest is one of the few not to have suffered the major depredations of tomb robbers — that of Tutankhamun which was discovered in 1922 by Howard Carter and Lord Carnarvon.

The tomb of Seti I is the deepest and perhaps the finest in the whole valley. It was discovered in October 1817 by Giovanni Belzoni, an Italian antiquity hunter who was financed in part by the British Consul — it was Belzoni who provided the British Museum with the head of Rameses II from the Ramesseum.

The tomb of Seti I has a rich collection of wall paintings from which these details are taken. That above features Osiris, Lord of the Underworld.

the contrary, it seemed to lead to an increasingly democratic afterlife, and thus a general intensification of religious observance and practice. Osiris grew increasingly in stature, and through him access to eternity was no longer the exclusive domain of the pharaoh. From the Middle Kingdom onwards his cult had a profound effect on all levels of society, especially among the poor, who now through leading a righteous life in this world could earn a place in the next one and, after the Day of Judgement, become an Osiris himself.

Each man at his death faced a tribunal of 42 assessor gods. He would be required to deliver the Negative Confession — denying to each god in turn that he had committed any serious crimes during his lifetime. After this ordeal, further interrogation took place in the presence of Thoth, the impartial recorder of the gods, Ma'at, the Goddess of Truth, and Anubis, the God of Embalming. The deceased's heart sat in one pan of the Scales of Justice and Ma'at's Feather of Truth in the other. The Goddesses of Fate and Destiny then gave their testimony and, if found innocent, the deceased's heart would balance the scales; he would be declared free from sin and his soul would pass through into the realm of Osiris. If the scales did not balance, then the deceased was considered guilty, and Ammut, the 'Devouress' or 'Eater of the Dead' — a hybrid monster part crocodile, part hippo and part lion — would devour the heart, thus bringing about the complete destruction of the deceased's soul, which therefore forfeited any hope of a continued existence in the afterlife.

The land of Osiris was of a similar structure to this world, but full of abundance and contentment; an idealised place of eternal springtime. There the pharaohs were in union with the gods, the rich and noble passed their time in continued luxury and the poor farmed. Osiris's main temple-shrine at Abydos became a great centre of pilgrimage for the living, and tombs were equipped with model boats for the souls of those who hadn't made the pilgrimage when alive, to sail to Abydos when dead.

ABOVE: Detail of a wall painting from the temple of Amun at Karnak. It is from the paintings in tombs and temples that most of our knowledge of ancient Egyptian religion, myth and legend is garnered, for it is in these tombs that a society without a substantial written culture left its 'texts'.

The prevalence and quality of tombs in the nomes in this period indicate a decline in both the concrete and abstract power of the pharaoh, and reflect the evolution of religious belief as well as decentralisation of power.

But with the emergence of the New Kingdom, central power asserted itself, again at Thebes, and a new royal god was composed of Amun and Re', with his own creation myth. His priesthood grew very powerful, as the spoils of empire were heaped on Amun-Re' by the pharaohs who credited their success to him, and sewed the seeds of their own eventual decline, as the priesthood of the god became autonomous and hereditary, and finally controlled all Upper Egypt and founded a dynasty. The evolution of Amun-Re', and Akhenaten's attempt at monotheism with Aten, reflect the power-politics between the upper echelons of ancient Egyptian society — the pharaoh on one hand and the priesthood on the other. Religious life for the peasant bulk of the population remained pretty much as it was, centring on Osiris with his fertility and afterlife aspects; Bes, the grotesquely humorous dwarf-god of love and marriage; Tauret, his hippopotamus wife, responsible for fecundity and childbirth; and local, popular zooamorphic gods. Isis too was worshipped as the sustaining mother-goddess, and Thoth, the god of wisdom, crafts and magic, knowledgeable and helpful. Later, in the Ptolemaic period, the Greek and Egyptian religions fused in the aspect of animal worship. There was a long tradition of animal worship in both cultures, and this was augmented by the creation of the bull-god Serapis, and by a big increase in the ceremonial burials of the animal sacred to the god of a particular area, in special catacombs within temple precincts.

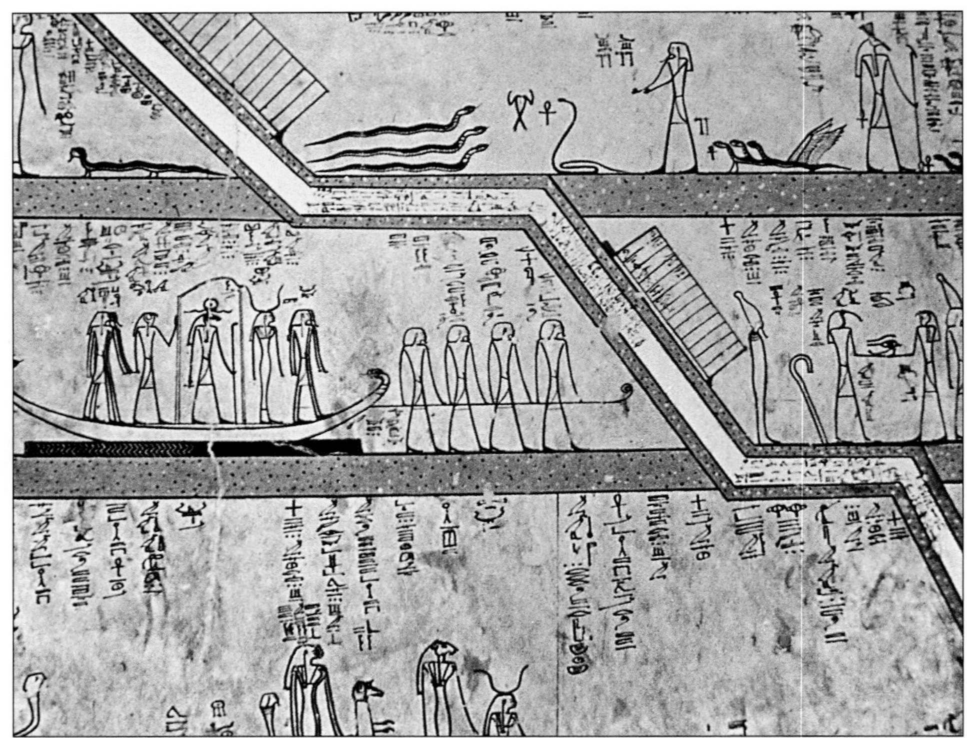

RIGHT: Detail from a wall painting in the tomb of Thutmose III in the Valley of the Kings. Tuthmose III was one of the great warrior kings of the New Kingdom who reconquered territory in Palestine and fought in Syria.

BELOW: Detail from the Temple of Seti I at Abydos. Seti is making an offering to Hathor.

FAR RIGHT: Because of grave robbers and periods of lawlessness, many of the mummified bodies of the pharaohs were removed from their tombs and hidden in safe caches. For example in 1881 a cache was found in Deir el-Bahri cemetery which included Tuthmose III, Seti I and Rameses II and III. This is a detail from Deir el-Bahri.

Creation and the Great Myths

BELOW: Perhaps the most unusual aspect of Geb and Nut is the reversal of the normal sexual roles. The usually feminine earth becomes masculine and the male sky god a goddess. It was only when they were forcibly separated from their constant union at the command of Re' that the world came into being.

THERE are no complete primary sources for the Egyptian myths; in fact most of our knowledge of them comes secondhand, from the Greeks and Romans. There does not seem to have been the same emphasis on narrative within the religious culture, and no texts have been found that recount entire myths, but there are different native versions of episodes of particular ones. Presumably interpretation of the mythology was subject to the demands of the time, the location and the political motives of those who left their stories to posterity.

The most widespread creation myth is that of Re'-Atum — the sun-god with a bewildering array of names and aspects, who emerges from the dark primeval waters of Nun, creating light and the first land, a mound called the Benben. Re'-Atum then conceives the first generation of gods himself, spitting out or ejaculating Shu and Tefnut, deities of air and moisture. Setting the divine precedent that the pharaohs would mimic, brother and sister married and produced Geb and Nut, the Earth and the Sky; in their turn they gave birth to Osiris, Isis, Set and Nepthys.

These nine gods and goddesses are grouped together as the Great Ennead, and originated in Heliopolis, one of three great cities (the others were Memphis and Hermopolis) each of which had its own creation myth. Also in that pantheon was Horus, the son of Osiris and Isis; and the pharaoh was believed to be a earthly manifestation of him. In Memphis it was Ptah who emerged from the primeval mound. He was given a 'wife', Sakhmet, and a 'son', Nefertu, to make up the Memphite Triad, though Sokar, the God of the Memphite necropolis, is also linked with them. Apis was seen as a manifestation of Ptah, reflecting his legend that in

the form of celestial fire he impregnated a heifer to give birth to himself in the shape of a bull.

In Hermopolis, there was a set of eight deities — an ogdoad — representing primeval chaos before the coming of the sun-god. There were four frog-headed gods paired with four snake-headed goddesses: Nun and Naunet represented the primordial abyss; Heh and Hauet were a manifestation of infinity; Kek and Kauket personified darkness; and Amun and Amaunet were the essence of hidden power, omnipresent yet invisible. Reflecting the inherent duality of the Two Lands and its mythology, these male and female forms produced from themselves the mound out of chaos, upon which lay the egg containing the young sun-god Re'.

In Thebes, another great city destined to be the religious and political capital from the Middle Kingdom onwards, the creation myth centred on Amun. Once he had ousted Montu, the older god of the Theban Nome, Amun went on to combine with Re', the chief god of the Old Kingdom, and become the supreme god of the Egyptian pantheon. He was given a consort, Mut, and a son, Khons, to make the Theban Triad. The largest and most impressive Egyptian temples were raised in their names at Karnak and Luxor.

At Elephantine Khnum was said to have created life on his potter's wheel. He too had a consort, Satis, and Anukis made up the triad, as their divine child.

All these sets of gods have no family connection, but act as a family model. Through a process of syncretism over a long period of time they combine and coalesce in new incarnations. Thus Re' and Amun and Atum are put together in an endless variety of formats, and all the gods have this ability to regenerate and

ABOVE: In myth it was at Edfu that Horus pierced Set during their battle.

It is unsurprising, therefore, that there is a major temple to Horus in Edfu, where (RIGHT) this colossal granite statue of Horus as a falcon — once one of a pair — stands at the doorway to the Hypostyle Hall (Hypostyle means that the roof is held up by columns or pillars). The Temple of Horus at Edfu is one of the best preserved of all Egyptian religious buildings.

Horus wears the double crown of united Egypt, thus stressing his close connection with the pharaoh — the pharaoh was said to be the physical manifestation of Horus on earth.

There are other statues of Horus at Edfu; this one (LEFT) is in front of the massive pylon.

renew, reflecting the ancient Egyptians' veneration of the past — their archaism.

Just as there were many creator-god myths, so too with the solar cycle myths; with the same essential imagery and motifs yet endless variation. The meaning was the cycle itself. The sun-god was born anew each dawn, and crossed the sky in his solar barque, gradually ageing and finally dying (although this is never mentioned). He then travels during the night through the Underworld, in a cycle of regeneration. The personnel and the equipment in his barque change frequently, from abstract aspects of his being to other gods and other manifestations. During the day Re' was manifested in hawk-headed form, his boat called 'Mandjet' invisibly towing the 'boat of millions', containing all the souls of the deceased. At night for his regenerative journey through the Underworld, Re' was manifested in ram-headed form. His boat was now called 'Mesektet', towed by jackals and snakes with Set at the prow, who defended and protected it from Apophis — the deadly indestructible serpent who attempted to swallow the whole boat each evening at the entrance to the Underworld.

One of the main mythological cycles is that of Osiris, which was closely interwoven with the evolution of the Two Lands, and the institution of divine kingship, and probably reflects and interprets actual past events. Osiris was the acknowledged heir of Atum, married to his sister Isis. But his brother Set was jealous of him and, inviting him to a banquet under the guise of friendship, imprisoned Osiris in a chest, which was then thrown into the Nile. The chest drifted downriver to Byblos, where it lodged in the branches of a tree. Isis, who had been searching everywhere, found the chest and hid it in the marshes of the delta; but Set discovered it once again whilst out hunting and, angrily breaking it open, he cut the body of Osiris into pieces, scattering them far and wide. But Isis called her sister Nepthys to help her collect all the pieces together and make the first mummy. Despite her great magic powers, Isis could not bring Osiris back to life, yet she managed to impregnate herself on him in the form of a hawk, and gave birth to Horus. Set discovered what had taken place and hoped to murder Horus too, but Isis invoked the protection of Re', who sent Thoth to arbitrate. Osiris remained a king, but king of the Underworld.

When Horus became a man, he claimed his father's rank and inheritance, and aspired to leadership of the gods, but Set contested his claim and challenged him. Re' favoured Set, but most of the other Gods preferred Horus, and so Re' retired from the debate in a bad temper. Eventually battle ensued between Horus and Set, and being older and more experienced, Set began to dominate. But he lacked an ally equal to the one Horus could call on — the great Isis — who was determined her son would come into his inheritance. She guided him through all the stages of the struggle, yet still he could not completely vanquish Set, so in the end all the gods decided to appeal to Osiris himself. Osiris rebuked them and championed his son as his rightful heir, and so Horus finally came to his inheritance. The pharaoh came to be seen as the incarnation of Horus alive, and Osiris in death, although as time went by Osiris-hood was open to any pure heart. Other versions of this myth have Osiris and Set ruling over separate parts of the country, but Set mismanages his part, which turns to desert, and he decides to do away with Osiris and have it all, thus leading to their conflict. Both Set and Horus did many vile things to each other in their struggle for dominance — rape, castration, amputation, blinding, as well as various less harmful tricks to try and outwit each other. Horus even savagely attacked his mother Isis, when she prevented him from finishing Set off when he had the chance. Although there are many versions of their struggle, all these Horus-Set myths end with arbitration from Thoth, and a collective decision on the part of all the gods in favour of Horus.

RIGHT: The Tomb of Seti I boasts some of the finest funerary paintings in Egypt. One of the most spectacular images is the burial chamber's astronomical ceiling.

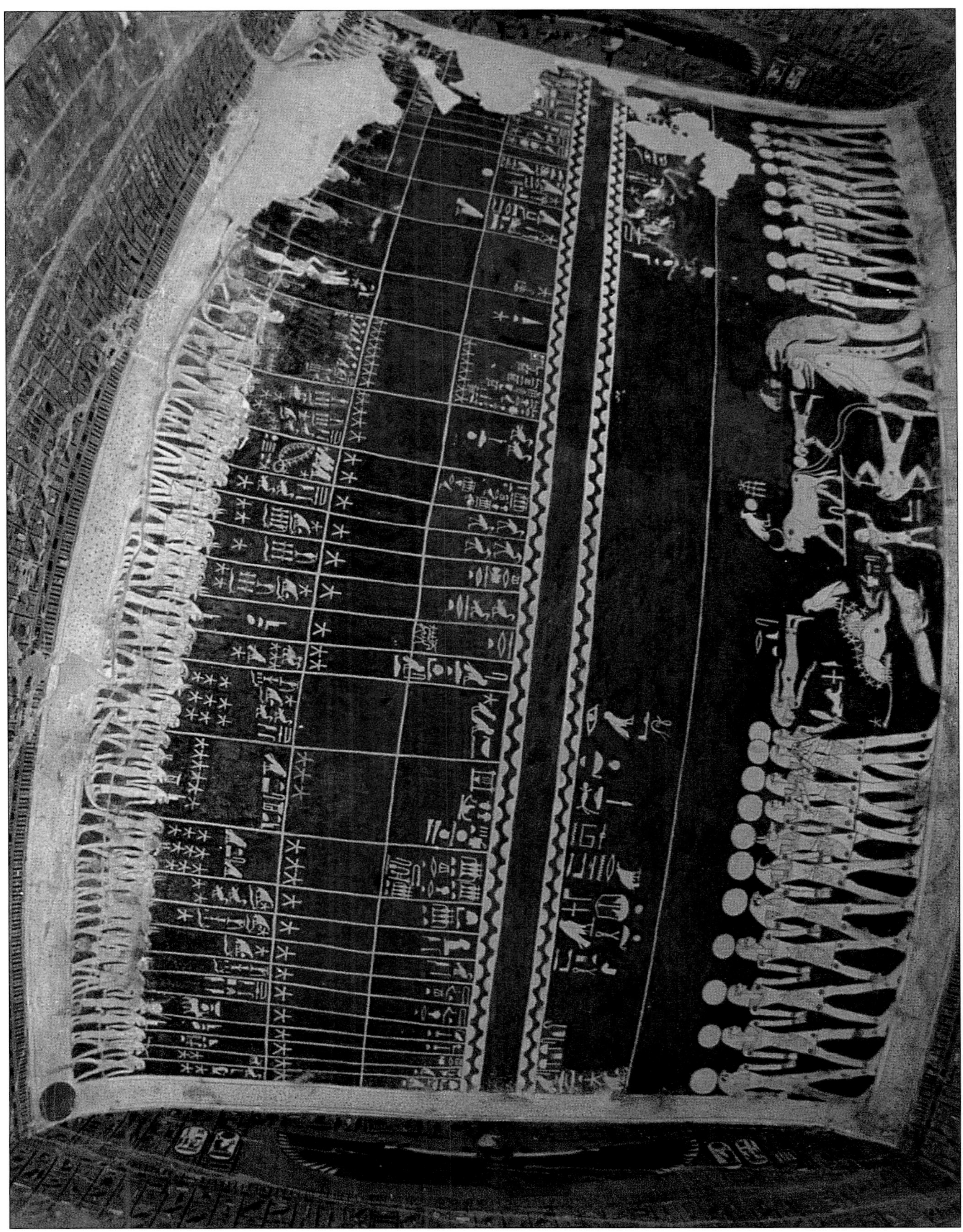

Mummification and Burial

ALONG with pyramid building, mummification is the most famous skill of the Ancient Egyptians. It is a method of preserving artificially the bodies of dead people and animals. It evolved from the natural effect of desiccation that happened in the first simple graves of the pre-dynastic period. Bodies placed in shallow graves and covered with sand survived very well because of the arid atmosphere and intense heat. When graves became more elaborate with coffins and vaults, these natural conditions changed and necessitated the development of preservation techniques and complicated ceremonies to ensure survival in the next world. Mummification took place in workshops attached to the necropolis, which also supplied most other funerary equipment. Methods varied according to the time, the location and the wealth of the deceased.

By the 5th Dynasty internal organs were being removed, with only the heart left in place. Vacant cavities were filled, and the outer wrappings were saturated in resin so that the features could be carefully modelled and then emphasised with paint. In contrast to earlier pre-dynastic burials, the body was laid in an extended position. By the time of the New Kingdom methods had evolved, with better preservative techniques on the tissues. The whole process took 70 days, and the most vital part was the dehydration of the body in natron — a naturally occurring preservative.

Firstly the brain was extracted, sometimes through the nose, but also through an incision in the skull. Next the viscera were removed through an incision in the left side, and then the cavities were sterilised. The viscera were treated separately with natron, then dried and molten resin was applied. (Eventually the viscera and other parts were stored in Canopic jars, each guarded by a son of Horus and a protective goddess.) The body was now temporarily packed with natron and fragrant resins, before being immersed in natron for about 70 days. When this time had passed, the temporary packing materials were removed and sand and clay were used to bulk out the limbs just underneath the skin. Next the body cavities were filled with resin-soaked linen, and bags of fragrant materials, herbs and incense. Finally the body was anointed with unguents and bandaged up, with the inclusion of protective amulets and jewellery, and the outside of the bandages were often painted with a likeness of the deceased.

At the end of the 70-day period, and just prior to burial, a ceremony was carried out called the Opening of the Mouth, in which the mummy was magically brought back to life. The mummy was then placed in a coffin, often anthropoid in shape, and again its image was painted on the front. For the great pharaohs and nobles there was often a huge outer stone sarcophagus. Within coffins and on the walls of tombs were painted and written texts and spells to aid in the afterlife — the coffin and pyramid texts, and the Egyptian Book of the Dead. Eyes were painted on the sides so that all things within the tomb could be activated by the owner. Other items of funerary equipment included funerary statuettes, called Ushabti figures. The purpose of these was to have an avatar who could carry out any of the deceased's drudgery or unpleasant work in the next life. Sometimes there would also be a life-size wooden statue of the deceased, or else a painting, so that the soul could inhabit these when necessary to obtain sustenance and move around, making use of the many grave goods, with their replica back-up images.

In the afterlife with the gods, the owner of the tomb still had his own place, where he could rest and revive, before returning to the celestial environment. The Ancient Egyptian word for pyramid (which is Greek) is 'mer', meaning Place of Ascension. Most mummies in the delta area of Lower Egypt have not survived, due to the climactic conditions. But in the much more arid valley area of Upper Egypt a large number has survived in very good condition and give us first-hand evidence of these complicated burial techniques.

ABOVE: Tutankhamun's quartzite sarcophagus and its granite lid; it originally contained three coffins. Famously discovered in the Valley of the Kings by Howard Carter in 1922 to world-wide fascination, the discovery of Tutankhamun's relics provoked a renewed interest in all things Egyptian, as it was one of the few tombs found intact and unmutilated by centuries of grave robbers, despite having been robbed twice.

Who Was Who in Ancient Egypt

Aah An anthropomorphic moon god, a manifestation of Thoth. He was depicted wearing the moon symbol, a combination of the full and crescent moons.

Aken Custodian of the ferry-boat in the Underworld.

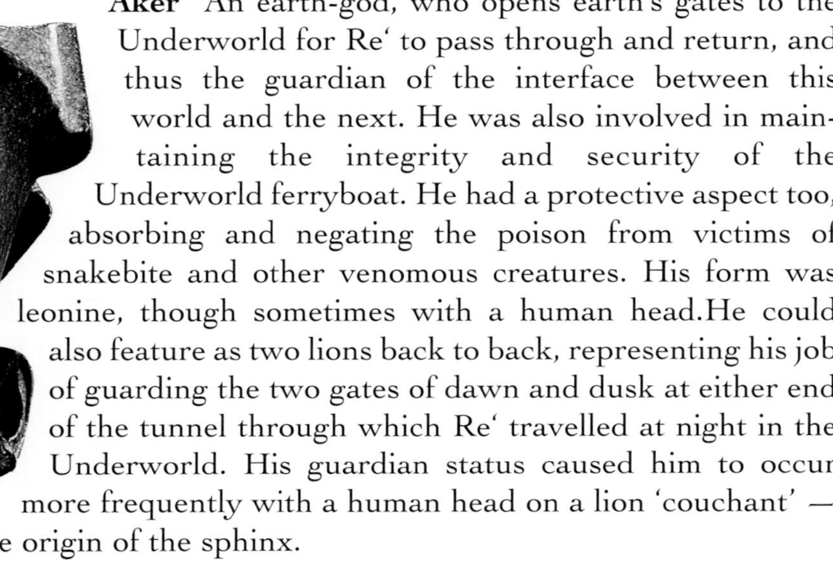

ABOVE: Amun from the Temple of Mut at south Karnak. The temple was founded by Amenhotep III on the site of an earlier temple. Christie's Images

Aker An earth-god, who opens earth's gates to the Underworld for Re' to pass through and return, and thus the guardian of the interface between this world and the next. He was also involved in maintaining the integrity and security of the Underworld ferryboat. He had a protective aspect too, absorbing and negating the poison from victims of snakebite and other venomous creatures. His form was leonine, though sometimes with a human head.He could also feature as two lions back to back, representing his job of guarding the two gates of dawn and dusk at either end of the tunnel through which Re' travelled at night in the Underworld. His guardian status caused him to occur more frequently with a human head on a lion 'couchant' — the origin of the sphinx.

Amaunet Consort of Amun. Symbol of protection. Amaunet was the female counterpart of Amun in the creation myth of the Hermopolitan ogdoad. When Amun was elevated to statehood she took second stage to Mut, his consort in the Theban Triad.

Amenhotep Courtier, royal scribe and sage of the 18th Dynasty, Amenhotep was deified in the Ptolemaic period, one of the few commoners to be awarded this honour for his outstanding achievements. He was the foremost official of Amenhotep III, and as such was involved in the whole gamut of state business, from temple design and construction to military recruitment. His cult was confined to Thebes, and it was as royal scribe that he was most revered.

Am-Heh A dangerous Underworld god, with the face of a dog. Only Amun could cope with Am-Heh, to anyone else he was lethal.

Ammut Underworld goddess — Devouress of the Dead. Part crocodile-lioness-hippo, her job was to swallow the heart of anyone who did not pass the judgement of Ma'at, and was therefore unworthy to dwell in the realm of Osiris.

Amun, Amon, Ammon, Amen Supreme creator-god. The 'hidden one'. Amun was the manifestation of the eternal omnipresent creative power and energy that manifests itself in all living things; a god who cannot be seen — inscrutable and invisible to men and gods alike. God of Thebes. Ruler of the Theban Ennead. Protector of the Gods with his shadow. Amun had myriad forms; originally an air-god, he could assume other attributes; as Amun-kem-atef he was a snake deity; as Amun-kamutef, an ithyphallic, fertility god. At Karnak he was portrayed as a sacred ram, a symbol of procreative power; the Nile goose was another animal sacred to him, as was the lion. His fertility and regenerative powers could range from the sexual to the agricultural. His importance grew with Thebes after he had ousted Montu, the Theban war-god. By the time of the 18th Dynasty Amun, as patron of the pharaohs, combined with Re' and became predominant, the chief god of Egypt. Yet during the same dynasty he was almost overthrown (see *Akhenaten)*. He came to lasting prominence with the Theban-led 19th Dynasty of Rameses II, when Egypt was the supreme ancient power, and the great temples raised to him at Luxor and Karnak were some of the most impressive and finest works of the Ancient Egyptian culture, and of antiquity. From the Middle Kingdom onwards his name was incorporated into those of various pharaohs, and during the periods of expansion and empire he was attributed with great military prowess, manifested through the pharaoh. Though king of the gods, Amun was esteemed amongst the poor as a protective deity, to whom they could appeal for fair play against corruption and manipulation from those above them, as aid against venomous creatures, and protection on long journeys.

ABOVE: Akhenaten succeeded to the throne in 1379BC as Amenhotep IV. He changed his name early in his reign and, helped by his powerful wife Nefertiti, tried to dispense with the old pantheon of gods, concentrating on Aten. There seems little doubt that this was part of a political struggle between his family and the priesthood and that he had the help of the military in this project, for he attempted to have the word Amun and all references to the plural 'gods' destroyed — a massive task. He was succeeded by the boy king Tutankhamun and his monotheism and his capital, el-'Armana, were dismantled. Christie's Images

Anhur Sky-war-god, popular in 18th-24th Dynasties. Creative power of the sun, and warlike aspect of Ra. Popular with ordinary peasants.

Andjety Precursor of Osiris. Closely related to the monarch. Appeared as a ram-headed man — a symbol of fertility.

Anti Sky-hawk-god associated with Horus. He protected the regions of the east, where the sun-god rose.

Anubis Anthropomorphic jackal-headed god of cemeteries, mummification and embalming. Son of Osiris, Anubis brought the souls of the dead before the judges of the infernal regions and led them into the land of Osiris after they had passed that test. He anointed the body after death and protected it from desecration. He invented mummification when he embalmed the body of Osiris, and bound it up in the bandages woven by Isis and Nephthys — so well that it resisted all decay. He was hailed as god of the western desert, with its implications of death, burial and the afterlife.

Anuket, Anukis, Anket Goddess of the cataracts of the lower Nile. Dual-tempered, she was embracer or strangler. Her sacred animal was the gazelle. In the New Kingdom she was designated the role of divine child of Khnum and Satis.

ABOVE: Anubis was more often portrayed anthropomorphically, with only a jackal's head. But the whole jackal itself with its associations of death and desert was seen to be a living manifestation of Anubis, who came to be the most prominent of all jackall gods.

Apis Ancient bull-god, manifestation of Ptah, creator-god of Memphis, for whom he was a mediator between himself and mankind, and consulted as an oracle. Also identified with the pharaoh as a symbol of kingship and strength. The Apis bulls were kept and worshipped at Memphis, close to the Temple of Ptah. Upon death they were mummified and buried with great ceremony at the Serapeum — a huge underground complex in the Memphite necropolis at Saqqara. At death Apis became linked with Osiris, the origin of the Ptolemaic hybrid Serapis.

Apophis A huge and indestructible snake-god, symbolising chaos, whose lethal powers are directed against the sun-god, and who every night was defeated in order that the sun-god could shine again upon the earth.

Assessor Gods 42 Underworld deities who assessed the earthly life of the dead. Each one was associated with a particular sin or crime, and to each one in turn the deceased had to deny involvement, known as the Negative Confession.

Aten A manifestation of the creator-sun-god Re', invisible to man. In an official revolution Akhenaten (Amenhotep IV) forced him into a monotheistic position. Yet in a way the exclusive worship of Aten was the climax of a religious quest by the pharaohs of the 18th Dynasty for an ultimate god, all-powerful and omnipresent. It was also a way to curb the power of the Theban priesthood at Karnak. But it went entirely against the grain of a polytheistic culture, and lasted no longer than its prime instigator. Aten was an aspect of the sun-creator, literally meaning 'disk', and was portrayed as such, with an Uraeus — the cobra goddess of royal insignia — and rays emanating from the disc's lower arc ending in hands, some holding Ankh, the hieroglyph for 'life'. Aten as a manifestation of the sun-god occurred far back in history, prior to his brief ascension in the New Kingdom, but it was in this period that he began to be associated with royalty and have an active cult under their patronage. Given the power and autonomy of the priesthood of Amun-Re' at the time, one can sense a motive behind the pharaoh's promotion of Aten, to offset that power. When Akhenaten moved the capital from Thebes, he built a new one which he called Akhetaten and, in keeping with his religious revolution, he encouraged a similar revolutionary approach in the arts. He himself was depicted in this new distinctive and realistic style, the only known break from the tradition, illustrating how closely linked state art was with religious beliefs. When Akhenaten died, he and the cult of Aten were expunged from the history of the Two Lands.

Atum Anthropomorphic creator-sun-god of Heliopolis, the paramount centre of sun-worship in Ancient Egypt, who combined with Re' to make the supreme solar deity and father of the Heliopolitan Ennead. Atum willed himself into being, and went on to make the universe in the form of Shu — air — and Tefnut — moisture, through masturbation or expectoration. They in turn made Geb — earth — and Nut — sky. The story goes that Geb and Nut were making love when they were separated at Atum's command. Nut, on top, arced her back upwards to form the sky; Geb formed the earth. Atum was seen as the father of the pharaoh, to whom the pharaoh returned and depended on for protection after death. The lion, the bull, the snake and the lizard were all sacred to Atum.

Babi An extremely fierce, bloodthirsty Underworld baboon god, associated with male virility. A testosterone nightmare, Babi lived on those judged unfit for the realm of Osiris, and was capable of murder on sight, though he did have a protective aspect too against snakes and other dangers.

Banebdjedet, Ba Neb Tetet, Banebdedet, Banaded Ram-god of Mendes in the north-east of the delta. Associated with Khnum. Level-headed arbiter among the gods. When Horus and Set were at an impasse, it was Banebdjedet who paved the way towards arbitration, by recommending the goddess Neith be consulted. Though

ABOVE: Bes — benign dwarf-god, guardian of the family and conjugal union. He particularly looked after women especially at childbirth when he provided protection from evil spirits. He is also closely associated with dancing and music and is sometimes depicted wearing a lion or leopard skin indicating his possibly Sudanese origins. From the Roman birth house in the Temple of Hathor at Dendera.

BELOW: Hapy — the god of the Nile in flood (inundation) hence the god of fucundity. He is recognised by the crest of papyrus on his head and the gifts he bears, however he is always shown as an hermaphrodite. Christie's Images

Banebdjedet preferred the claim of Set, Neith found in favour of Horus.

Bastet, Bas, Bast Feline-sun-goddess of Bubastis, daughter of the sun-god. She became very popular, especially in Ptolemaic times. Bubastis was the ancient capital of Lower Egypt, and Bastet was an ancient deity, made a state one when the 22nd Dynasty made her city the capital. She was first represented as a woman with a lioness's head, holding a sistrum or rattle, but later a cat's head replaced that of the lioness. She originally was a manifestation of the anger of Re' but her nature softened, and in the Ptolemaic period she was a goddess of pleasure, and consequently much more popular. In her temples cats were kept and at death were mummified and buried in catacombs (although there is no reason to suppose that this is the etymological starting point for that word! — in fact catacombs has a latin root). Bastet had a son, the lion-headed Mihos. She was closely linked to the king as nurse and protectress, and was identified and confused with Mut and Sekhmet.

Bes Grotesque but benign dwarf-god. Protector of childbirth. Guardian of the night. In contrast to the other gods, Bes was considerably less than immaculate. Hairy, bandy-legged, plump, his good nature and love of fun and music made him popular with the poor and he became universal as a protective deity of the family and conjugal union, as well as against dangerous animals and the night. He was also the god of cosmetics and female adornment, and utensils in general.

Cavern deities Punishers of the Underworld.

Duamutef One of the four sons of Horus. A jackal-headed funerary god responsible for the stomach. (*See Sons of Horus.*)

Geb Earth-god, son of Atum, president of the divine tribunal on kingship in the dispute between Horus and Set; and just as he vindicated the claim of Horus, so does he support the ruling pharaoh. In his role as an earth-god of fertility Geb appeared green-coloured and sometimes ithyphallic. Perhaps his most interesting point is that Geb is a male earth figure, it being much more common in ancient cultures to view the earth as female. (*See Amun.*)

The Great Ennead Pantheon of nine gods originating in Heliopolis, the ancient religious capital of Egypt. Consisting of Atum-Re', the sun-creator-god and his descendants: Shu, Tefnut, Geb, Nut, Osiris,

Isis, Set, Nephthys and Horus. (*See Creation and the Great Myths.*)

Ha Anthropomorphic guardian-god of the desert, in the west and the oases.

Hapi Personification of the waters of the Nile, especially the inundation. Dwelling near the first cataract, Hapi is portrayed in well-fleshed anthropomorphic form, with a large paunch and pendulous breasts, suggesting plenty, and a crown of aquatic plants, often carrying a tray of food or pouring water from urns. Although he was featured in the reliefs of other deities' temples, Hapi had none of his own, and no priesthood.

Hapy One of the sons of Horus. A funerary god who protected the lungs after evisceration, assisted by the goddess Nephthys. (*See Sons of Horus.*)

Harpokrates Aspect of Horus — Horus-the-child. (*See Horus.*)

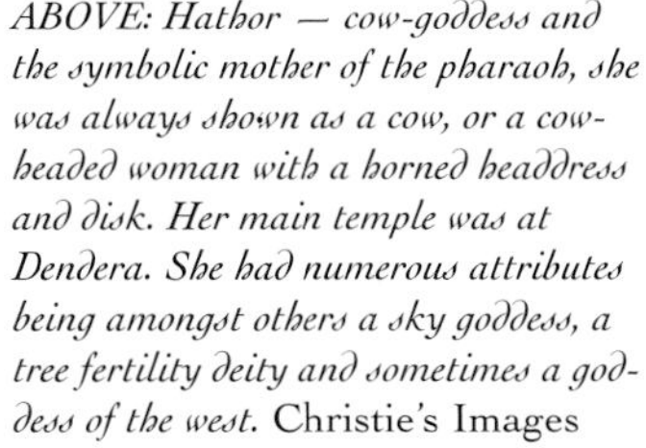

ABOVE: Hathor — cow-goddess and the symbolic mother of the pharaoh, she was always shown as a cow, or a cow-headed woman with a horned headdress and disk. Her main temple was at Dendera. She had numerous attributes being amongst others a sky goddess, a tree fertility deity and sometimes a goddess of the west. Christie's Images

Hathor Multi-aspected sky-cow goddess. Symbolic mother of the pharaoh. In funerary aspect as Lady-guardian of the western lands of the dead, she was protectress of the necropolis and the dead. Also goddess of destiny, healing, childbirth, love, music and dance, and protectress of women. When Re' became disgusted and disillusioned with mankind, he ordered Hathor to destroy all men. She set about her task with such fury and zeal that he had second thoughts, and had to resort to trickery in order to stop her. Despite this frightening negative capability, Hathor was predominantly a benign mother-goddess. She was portrayed as a cow, or as a woman with cow's horns; she could also be represented as a lioness, a snake or a sycamore. Her main temples were at Dendera, Edfu and Ombos.

Hat-meyht Fertility-fish goddess of Mendes in the delta, consort of Banebdjedet. Hat-meyt was represented in fish form.

LEFT: Detail of head and shoulders of Harpokrates — a Greek rendering of Horus the child, usually depicted on his mother Isis' knee (See photograph page 33). Christie's Images

Heh Anthropomorphic personification of infinity.

Heket Ancient goddess of childbirth, creation and grain germination, she took the form of a frog or frog-headed woman.

Heryshaf Ram-god of mid-Egypt. Personification of Re'. Also associated with Osiris. His city of Hnes was the capital of Northern Egypt during the first Intermediate period, and it was at this time that his association with Re' and Osiris was promulgated. Heryshaf was portrayed as a man with a ram's head.

Hesat Cow-milk-goddess; gave birth to the king as a golden calf.

Hetepes-sekhus Underworld cobra-goddess. Eye of Re'. She destroyed the souls of Osiris's enemies, with an army of crocodiles.

Horus Many-aspected, falcon-headed, sky-sun-god. Son of Osiris and Isis, who fought Set to reclaim his father's inheritance. (*See The Great Ennead.*) His hawk's head insignia was used far back in pre-dynastic times, as a symbol of identity and leadership. Horus could be portrayed as either a hawk, or a hawk-headed man. The unification of the Two Lands saw him ascendant — merging with other deities to become a state god at Memphis. He was a symbol of unification, strength, divine kingship (the pharaoh is Horus alive), perfection, protection (the Eye of Horus), and purification; some of his manifestations are listed below:

Harpokrates — Horus the child = child of Osiris and Isis.

Haroeris, Harwer — Horus the Elder; mature, claiming his father's throne, fighting Set.

Harakhty — Horus of the horizon = Sun god.

Harsiesis — Horus son of Isis = Avenger of Osiris.

Harsomtus — Horus of the Two Lands = Uniter of Upper and Lower Egypt.

Harendotes — Horus father-protector = Battling against Set.

ABOVE: Isis — a crucial figure in the pantheon, symbolic mother of the king and one of the great mother-goddesses of mythology, she is sister-wife of Osiris, one of the children of Geb and Nut. Protector of the dead and guardian of the canopic jars, she wears on her head the cow horn crown and sun disc.
Christie's Images

Hu Personification of the royal authority. Hu was made from a drop of blood from the phallus of the sun-god Re'.

Imhotep Architect and courtier, designer and builder of the first Pyramid at Saqqara, which led to his deification, and adoption as a son of Ptah. Imhotep was revered as a god of learning, knowledge and healing. He was portrayed seated, with an open manuscript scroll on his knees, and with the shaven head of a priest.

ABOVE: Imhotep — the vizier of King Zozer, who was probably the architect of the Step Pyramid, the oldest stone building of its size in the world. He was deified as a son of Ptah for his work and later worshipped — particularly in Graeco-Roman times — as a god of medicine and as the founder of medical science in Egypt. Christie's Images

Ipy Kindly, protective hippo-goddess, associated with royalty.

Isis Great mother goddess of Egypt. The wife of Osiris, mother of Horus and the pharaoh. (*See The Great Ennead.*) Isis was an idealised woman and mother: loving, faithful, resourceful; she was the possessor of mind-boggling magical powers, the only person ever to discover the true name of the great sun god Re'. Her cult originated in Perehbet, and spread over the whole of Egypt. Her image is that of an attractive, mature woman, with a miniature throne on her head, or with cows' horns, the sundisk between them. The sistrum was sacred to her, and a magic knot called Tat. She was shown in many attitudes: suckling Horus the child, enthroned next to Osiris, and protecting both her husband and the souls of the dead with her winged arms. Her persistence and cunning were illustrated in the struggle between her son Horus and Set, when she caused Set to betray his sexual assault on Horus.

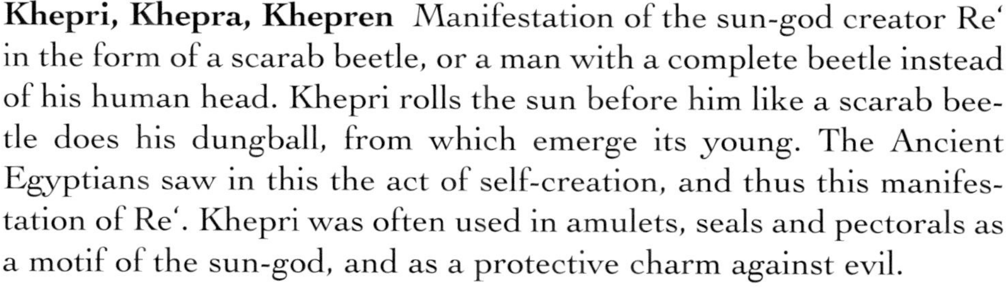

Khepri, Khepra, Khepren Manifestation of the sun-god creator Re' in the form of a scarab beetle, or a man with a complete beetle instead of his human head. Khepri rolls the sun before him like a scarab beetle does his dungball, from which emerge its young. The Ancient Egyptians saw in this the act of self-creation, and thus this manifestation of Re'. Khepri was often used in amulets, seals and pectorals as a motif of the sun-god, and as a protective charm against evil.

BELOW: Isis and Harpokrates — a Ptolemaic period statuette. Christie's Images

Kherty Earth ram-god with both hostile and protective capabilities. The pharaoh needed the power of Re' to protect him from Kherty, though in his positive aspect he could be the guardian of the royal tomb.

Khnum Ram-headed creator-god of Elephantine. He guards the source of the Nile, and controls the annual inundation. War-champion of the sun god Shu. In his capacity as guardian of the cataract region he was grouped with Satis and Anukis to make the Elephantine Triad, and, regarded as the soul of the sun-god, his name became Khnum-Re'. His other aspect was that of creator-god; linked to the procreative power of the ram and the life-giving waters of the Nile, Khnum was said to have made mankind, and indeed all life, on his potter's wheel.

ABOVE: Khons as a seated baboon. Khons is a lunar deity more usually shown as a man with the head of a falcon or with a disk on his head. He is the third member of the Theban triad, alongside Amun and Mut. Christie's Images

Khons, Khonsu Sky-moon-god. Son of Amun and Mut. One of the Theban Triad. Khons had various manifestations, ranging from a war-god to a god of healing. He is represented as a royal child, wearing the side plait (a sign of youth), and carrying the crook and flail. He is also shown as a falcon-headed youth surmounted by the lunar disk and crescent combined. His nature underwent a change from bloodthirsty war-god of the Old Kingdom, to divine child and healer in the New Kingdom. Khons had a temple dedicated to him in the precinct of Amun at Karnak.

Maahes A lion, or lion-headed god – the son of Re' and the cat-headed goddess Bastet. He was portrayed as a lion, or a lion-headed man.

Ma'at Personification and goddess of Truth and Justice, and cosmic harmony. Wife of Thoth. Ma'at's feather sat in the other scale, opposite the heart of the deceased, in judgement. Failure to balance the scales resulted in the most feared second death, and the loss of the possibility of the afterlife with Osiris in his kingdom. Ma'at was portrayed as a woman wearing an ostrich feather on her head, which could also by itself represent the goddess. The pharaohs saw Ma'at as their authority to rule, and are represented holding a miniature version of her in their hands, displaying their truthfulness and integrity to the major deities.

Mahaf Underworld ferryman. Also herald of the sun-god Re'.

Mehen Serpent god, protecting the sun-god's boat through its night-time journey in the Underworld. Mehen was usually portrayed coiled around the kiosk on the deck of the boat, in which Re' stood.

Mertseger Cobra-goddess of Thebes. Guardian of the royal tombs. She was portrayed as a coiled cobra, or as a cobra with the head of a woman, and had the reputation of being a dangerous but merciful goddess. Her abode was the peak of the mountain that overlooks the Valley of Kings in western Thebes.

Meskhent Goddess of childbirth and destiny. Meskhent ensured safe delivery, and then foretold the destiny of each child. She was portrayed as a woman with a headdress of palm shoots, or as a brick with a woman's head – representing the bricks with which women supported themselves when giving birth. After helping ensure a safe delivery, she would predict the future of the newly-born child.

Mesta, Imsety One of the four sons of Horus. He protected the liver after mummification. Mesta was represented as a bearded, mummiform man. He was aided in his task by Isis.

Min Anthropomorphic, ithyphallic god. The symbol of sexual procreativity and fecundity. Also combined with Horus as a protective deity of the eastern desert, roads and travellers. Min was seen as another manifestation of Amun, and wears his plumed headdress, holding a whip-like sceptre. He is also sometimes shown holding his erect phallus in his left hand. His sacred animal was the white bull, and his main centres were at Coptos and Panoplis.

Montu, Mont Falcon-headed war-god of Thebes and the Theban Nome. Montu was the embodiment of the martial vigour of the pharaoh, and as a war god was portrayed holding the khepesh — a curved sabre. Also manifested as a Buchis, a bull, kept in a shrine at Hermonthis. Montu was superseded by Amun at Thebes.

Mut Sky-war-goddess of Thebes.Wife of Amun. Symbolic mother of the pharaoh. Coalescent with Bastet. She was portrayed as a woman wearing a vulture headdress surmounted by the pshkent — the double crown of Egypt. She could also be lioness-headed, and hence her association with Bastet.

Nebethetepet Heliopolitan goddess. The feminine counterpart to the male creative principle of the sun-god Amun — the hand with which Atum brings the world into being.

Nefertum Son of Ptah and Sekhmet. The god of rebirth, symbolised by the lotus blossom. Nefertum was portrayed wearing a stylised lotus flower on top of his head and carrying the khepesh.

Nehebu-kau Invincible Underworld snake-god of protection. Represented as a snake but with human arms and legs, Nehebu-kau protected the pharaoh in the Underworld after death.

Neith Sky-creator-goddess of Sais, in the delta. Consort of Set. Goddess of war and weaving. Her red crown was absorbed into the crown of the pharaoh, the pshkent. Her oldest symbol is the shield with crossed arrows. It was claimed that Neith wove the world with her shuttle, and that Re' was her son.

RIGHT: Neith wearing the crown of Lower Egypt. One tradition has her mother of Isis, Osiris and Horus. Probably the original goddess of the delta, her cult was revived when Necho II (610-595BC) in the 26th Dynasty declared himself son of Neith. Christie's Images

Nekbet Vulture-goddess of Upper Egypt. Protector of mothers and children. She occurs as a heraldic device above the pharaoh, balancing the Lower Egyptian cobra-goddess, Wadjet. She was also represented as a vulture at rest. At royal births she was the protective nurse to the monarch.

Neper Agricultural god of grain. In manifestation Neper's body was dotted to represent corn. He represents agricultural prosperity and fecundity.

Nephthys, Nebthet Funerary-goddess of the Dead. Sister of Osiris and Isis. Consort of Set. She seduced Osiris and gave birth to Anubis. (*See The Great Ennead.*) She wears on her head the ideogram of her name: Neb, — a basket, and Het — a palace. Together with Isis she was a protectress of the Pharaoh in the Underworld. She could also take the form of a kite guarding the funerary bed of Osiris.

Nome Administrative unit in Ancient Egypt. (*See maps on pp44-47.*) The Nile was divided into 42 nomes and each had their own major city and god. The 22 nomes of Upper Egypt were fixed at least by the 5th Dynasty but the 20 of Lower Egypt had to wait for the Graeco-Roman period to become established. The nomes were strongly linked to the Nile and the Faiyum and the oases were not involved. 42 was a sacred number to the Egyptians — there were 42 Assessor gods and it is said that they had 42 sacred books.

BELOW: Osiris — god of the Underworld with his distinctive Atef crown which has a ram's horns and plumes. As judge of the dead and a universal god, cults in his name are found all over Egypt. Christie's Images

Nut Sky-goddess of the Heliopolitan Ennead. Daughter of Shu and Tefnut, Nut is represented as a slim-limbed girl, stretching up her body on her fingers and toes over her consort Geb. Like all Egyptian sky-goddesses, she could assume the form of a sacred cow. She was also thought to swallow the sun each evening, and give birth to it again each dawn. As a funerary deity she was believed to enfold the pharaoh in her soul at his death, so that he would dwell in the sky with her, and she provided sustenance for the dead in the Underworld.

Ogdoad Eight deities manifesting the primeval chaos before the coming of the sun-god. (*See Creation and the Great Myths.*)

Onuris Spear-carrying god of war and hunting. Onuris was portrayed as a bearded man wearing a crown of four high plumes. He was most frequently identified with Shu, but also Horus, whose cause he supported wholeheartedly. His consort was Mekhit, a lioness-headed woman whom he brought back from the south.

BELOW: Ptah is unmistakable in appearance with a skull cap, a sceptre in his hands combining 'ankh' — the symbol of life — with a djed column — a symbol of stability. Ptah was the creator god of Memphis and patron god of craftsmen. Christie's Images

Osiris Supreme god of the Underworld and the Dead. Firstborn of Geb and Nut. Murdered by his jealous brother Set. Counterpart to the sun-god below ground, and manifestation of the pharaoh after death. He brought civilisation to Egypt, and taught the people how to cultivate crops — hence also his manifestation as a grain god, as well his more usual funerary and mortuary incarnations. Osiris was portrayed in human form, mummified, holding the sceptres of kingship. He wore a crown which consisted of ram's horns and a tall centrepiece, with a plume on each side. His skin had a greenish tint. Osiris became increasingly important from the first Intermediate period onwards, offering as he did the chance of resurrection to any pure soul regardless of wealth or position. His main centre was at Abydos.

Pharaoh Egyptian kingship. The cult of divine ruler, deified through ritual. Warden of the Two Lands. Manifestation of Re', Horus and Osiris in human form.

Ptah Anthropomorphic creator-god of Memphis, part of the Memphis triad. Consort of Sekhmet. Father of Nefertem, he also adopted Imhotep. Apis, the sacred bull, was another manifestation. God of architects, artisans, artists and masons, he created the skills of design and sculpture. Ptah was represented as a shaven-headed mummiform man, holding a sceptre. He was most popular with the pharaohs of the 19th Dynasty. His funerary aspect was in combination with Sokar, the guardian of the Memphite necropolis, where he patented the life-restoring ceremony of The Opening of The Mouth. He was said to have created himself, and then spoken the universe into existence.

Qebehsenuef One of Horus's funerary sons. (*See Sons of Horus.*) He guarded the intestines after evisceration.

Re' Heliopolitan creator-sun-god. (*See the Great Ennead.*)The apex of all sun-god manifestations. Symbolised by a falcon with the sun on its head surrounded by a cobra, and by a scarab rolling the sun before him like a ball of dung. Also, in the Underworld, he became a ram-headed god. Combines or coalesces with other gods: Atum, Benu, Harakhti and Osiris. Re's

ABOVE: A bronze figure of Amun-Re', the supreme god of the Egyptian pantheon, wearing his complicated double-plumed crown symbolising his sun and sky origins. Christie's Images

cult escalated during the 5th dynasty and, after merging with Atum, he became the supreme solar deity. Re' was said to have created mankind from his tears, a symbolic birth, for mankind is nothing but a problem to the Gods, with his deceit, wickedness and violence. Finally Re' had enough and, becoming angry, he ordered Hathor to kill mankind. She took on the shape of Sakhmet and was so diligent in her task that Re' was shocked by the indiscriminate slaughter, and commanded her to stop. But Hathor-Sakhmet was so intent she ignored him, and he had to resort to trickery to stop her. By mixing beer with pomegranate juice he simulated blood, and left it on the battlefield. Hathor thought it was blood, and drank so much of it that she became drunk and unable to continue.

Renenutet Cobra-goddess of agriculture, protection, fertility and linen, especially bandages. Guardian of the Pharaoh. Renenutet was represented as a cobra rearing up to strike, or as an enthroned goddess. Embodying the role of divine motherhood, she was also portrayed as a woman suckling a child. Along with Shait she gave each child a destiny an allotted span of years, and she attended the weighing of men's hearts in the Hall of Two Truths. Her cult flourished in the fertile Faiyum, where she was connected to the Sobek.

Renpet Goddess of youth and springtime, but also fate and judgement. Renpet was linked with Time. She appeared as a woman with a palm-shoot on her head.

Sakhmet, Sekhmet Fierce lion-headed goddess of Memphis. Daughter of Re'. Consort of Ptah and one of the Memphis Triad. Hathor's instrument for the destruction of mankind, until Re' made her too drunk to continue. Sakhmet represented the destructive power of the sun, and was a daughter of Re'. But she also had a protective and healing side, and seemed happily married to Ptah — the most creative of the gods.

BELOW: Sekhmet — monumental granite head. A powerful goddess and daughter of Re', she was adopted by the pharaohs as the personification of fighting spirit. Christie's Images

Sarapis, Serapis The national god of Ptolemaic Egypt, combining Osiris and Apis. A god of the sun, fertility, healing and the afterlife.

Satis Goddess of the southern frontier. Consort of Khnum. Associated with the annual inundation. Satis was represented as a woman wearing the long white crown of Upper Egypt, with antelope horns or plumes.

Sepa Protective centipede-god from Heliopolis, Sepa had the power to prevent snakebites.

Serket, Selkis, Selket Protective scorpion-goddess, a daughter of Re'. She watched over the sky with Neith to prevent anyone interrupting Amun and his wife, and so became a guardian goddess of conjugal union. Selket was represented as a woman with a scorpion on her head, or as a scorpion with a woman's head. In her funerary aspect she was the helper and guard of Qebehsenuef, custodian of the viscera. She also helped the deceased orient themselves in the Underworld, and was believed to bind Apophis, the evil snake who was a manifestation of darkness and death. In the world of the living she was a kind of patron-saint for healers and witchdoctors, and a protective deity against venomous bites, and poison.

Seshat Horned-goddess of writing and archives, she was married to Thoth. It was Seshat who measured time, kept the royal accounts and helped the pharaoh with the the layout and foundations of temples. She also audited all the booty and tribute from foreign lands and military expeditions. She was shown as a woman wearing a panther skin robe, holding a pen, a palette and sometimes a tally-stick. On her head she wore a headband with a seven-pointed star on a stick.

BELOW: Selket, the scorpion goddess, is one of four goddesses who guard the coffin of Tutankhamun — the others being Neith at the north-east, Nephthys at the south-west and Isis (visible on left of photograph) at the north-west. Selket was at the south-east side.

Set, Seth, Setekh, Setesh, Suty, Sutekh God of chaos and disorder, thunder and storm, violence and the desert. Set was the second son of Geb and Nut, who tore himself out of his mother early. He was jealous of his brother Osiris and, killing him, usurped the throne, until he was finally ousted in favour of Horus. The personification of evil, Set was portrayed as a composite animal with four legs and an erect tail, and a gently curving snout. On his head rose two squared-off ears or horns; his skin was white and his hair red. He occurred more often anthropomorphically, with the head of this animal, whom the Greeks identified with their Typhon. Each month Set attacked and consumed the moon, the hiding place of Osiris, and preyed on the souls of the deceased, yet still Set was championed occasionally by various pharaohs, until he was adopted by the Hyksos invaders who settled in the delta. After their expulsion, Set's already battered reputation took a further drop, his statues were destroyed and his name became anathema. When he lost out to Horus, Set went to live with the sun-god, becoming his weather controller. He travelled with Re' in his solar boat and, standing in the prow, speared Apophis when he attacked. His two main centres of worship were Ombos and Kus.

ABOVE: Thoueris, or Taweret, Hippopotamus-bodied goddess of childbirth. (See page 42.) Christie's Images

Shay, Shait The personification of destiny. When the deceased reached the hall of judgement, Shay was present to give a true account of all sins and good works. Against her testimony there was no appeal.

Shezmu God of the winepress and other oils and unguents, Shezmu also had a bloodthirsty and dreadful aspect, when he sqeezes people's heads like grapes in his winepress, and binds up sinners to be led to slaughter. In early form he was anthropomorphic, but later on could be portrayed as a lion.

Shu Air-god of sunlight and the atmosphere. Husband of Tefnut, they made up the first couple of the Heliopolitan Ennead. At the command of Re' he forcibly separated Geb and Nut from their endless loving embrace, and held Nut up to make the sky. Shu was represented anthropomorphically, wearing a plume on his head and with his arms raised (supporting Nut). After Re', Shu was king of the world. But he was ambushed by the children of Apophis, and though he beat them he was left weakened and exhausted by the encounter. So he abdicated in favour of Geb, and retired to heaven. Shu had the usual dual aspect of punisher or protector, in the Underworld he was a very dangerous god who led a band of killers, and was a great peril for the deceased. In protective mode he could defend against Apophis and other demons.

Sia, Saa The personification of mind and intelligence, created by the blood dripping from the phallus of Re'. Aids the sun-god on board his boat during the night journey through the Underworld.

Sobek, Sebek, Suchos Crocodile-headed water-god, symbolising pharaonic might. Son of Neith, Sobek came to prominence in the 12th Dynasty when the delta was favoured. He originated in the Faiyum, though his temples were widespread, and he was linked to the evil god Set. His consort was Hathor, and their 'child' Khonsu. Though mainly portrayed anthropomorphically with a crocodile's head, he could also be a complete crocodile.

Sokar, Seker, Sokaris Hawk god, guardian of the Memphite Necropolis, Saqqara and the gate to the Underworld. In the Old Kingdom Sokar was seen as a manifestation of Osiris slain by Set, but he was more usually associated with Ptah, however by the Middle Kingdom this trio were linked in worship. But it was in his funerary aspect that Sokar was most important, his image occurring in many Theban royal tombs. He was shown anthropomorphically, with the head of a hawk, sometimes with horns and a crown.

Sons of Horus: Imsety, Hapy, Duamutef and Qebehsenuef The four funerary gods responsible for protecting the internal organs that were removed, embalmed, and kept in Canopic jars, the stoppers of which were fashioned in their images. (*See Mummification and Burial.*)

Imsety was anthropomorphically portrayed, he looked after the liver and was watched over in turn by Isis.

Hapy was represented as a baboon, his province was the lungs, and his guardian goddess was Nephthys.

Duamutef was interpreted as a jackal, he guarded the stomach and was protected by Neith.

Qebehsenuef, who took the form of a hawk, had the intestines under his jurisdiction. Serket was his guardian goddess.

ABOVE: Wadjet, the cobra goddess of Lower Egypt whose main centre was at Buto. (See page 43.) Christie's Images

Sopedu, Septu, Sopd Falcon border-patrol god, protector of the Eastern Desert. Linked with Horus. Sopedu the 'Smiter of Asiatics' was portrayed as a man with foreign features, wearing two feathers on his head, or as a falcon wearing the same feathers. In his cosmic

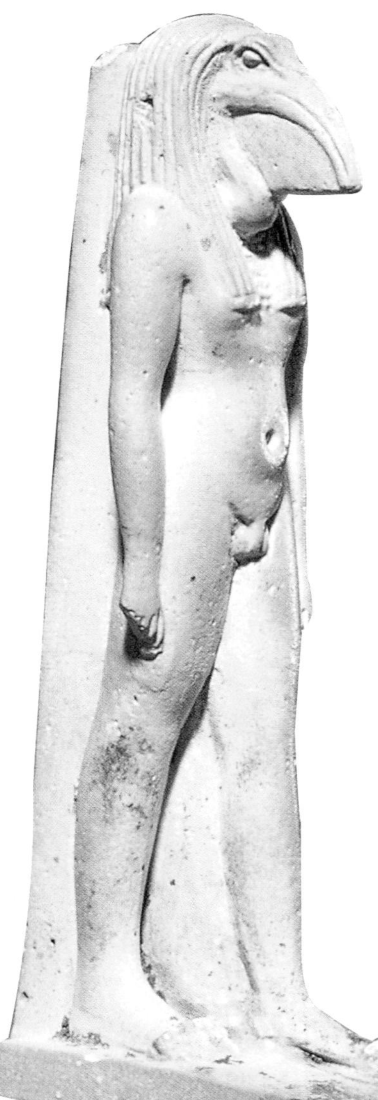

ABOVE: Composite figure of Ibis-headed Thoth with lion's paw feet: Thoth was the god of wisdom. His cult centre was at Hermopolis — the modern el-Ashmunein. Christie's Images

aspect Sopedu combines with another hawk-deity, Horus. His area of influence included the turquoise mines of the Sinai Peninsula, though his main centre was in the north-eastern delta.

Sothis, Sopdet Goddess personifying Sirius, the star that hearald ed the annual inundation. This astral deity sired Sopedu with Orion. She was portrayed as a woman wearing a tall conical crown with the Uraeus, and a five-sided star on top.

Souls of Pe and Nehken Gods who symbolised the pre-dynastic rulers of the Two Lands prior to unification: Pe or Buto in the delta, and Nehken or Hierakonopolis in Upper Egypt. They were considered the protective ancestors of the living pharaoh. Those of Pe were visualised with the heads of falcons, and those of Nehken with the heads of jackals.

Ta-bitjet Protective scorpion goddess, the wife of Horus.

Tatenen, Tanen, Tathenen Personification of the very fertile Nile silt, left after the waters of the annual inundation. In this aspect of fertility-deity Tatenen was combined with Geb. He also combined with Ptah in a creator-god mode, and was guardian of the royal dead. Tatenen was portrayed as a man with a crown consisting of two feathers and two ram's horns.

Taweret, Tauret, Thoueris Protective hippopotamus goddess. Along with her consort Bes the dwarf-god, Taweret was the protector of women in pregnancy and childbirth. Very popular with the ordinary people, like her husband she had a bizarre appearance — a female hippopotamus with human breasts, lion's feet, and a crocodile's back and tail. She wore a wig of straight hair that fell to her shoulders. Her alarming appearance belied her benign nature, and frightened off malevolent spirits.

Tayet Goddess of weaving and, in funerary aspect, of linen bandages used in embalming and mummification.

Tefnut Primeval sky-goddess of moisture. Consort of Shu. One of the Heliopolitan Ennead. Eye of Re'. Goddess of dew, rain and mist, Tefnut could assume leonine form or remain anthropomorphic, except for her lioness's head.

Thoth Moon-god of data, Thoth is credited with inventing writing, the calendar, science, music, magic and art, medicine, maths and astronomy. The Divine Recorder; conciliator and arbiter among the Gods. Thoth was the divine regulative force, present throughout the funeral rites, involved in the judgement of the soul. He was a staunch supporter of Horus, but healed the wounds of both gods after their combat. Thoth displaced the eight creator-deities of Hermopolis to become paramount — hailed as a creator-god in his own right. He was depicted anthropomorphically with the head of an ibis, or just as an ibis, or as a baboon. In each case on his head he wore the combined lunar disc and crescent. He was esteemed particularly by scribes, and gave the knowledge of hieroglyphs to man.

Wadjet, Uajyt Cobra-goddess of the delta. Preserver of the royal authority. Along with her southern counterpart, Nehkbet, she was part of the royal insignia, protecting the pharaoh — the Uraeus cobra of the Double Crown. Her cult centre was at Buto, also known as Pe. Wadjet is depicted as a cobra rearing up as if ready to strike. In her role as eye of Re', she could also be portrayed as a lioness.

Wadjwer Aquatic-fertility god of procreation and prosperity. Wadjwer was represented anthropomorphically — well-fleshed and well fed. He originated in and personified the delta.

Weneg A son of Re', Weneg personified cosmic order, and was thus the judge of other gods, and a male counterpart to Ma'at.

Wepawawet Jackal-headed god of Upper Egypt. Wepawawet lived in the west and was the guide of the dead, leader of expeditions, and war-champion of the pharaoh. He was identified with Horus. Wepawawet also guarded the sun boat of Re' on its nightly journey through the Underworld. He was represented anthropomorphically, with a jackal's head, and often dressed as a soldier, carrying various insignia.

BELOW: Wepawawet: the opener of the ways — guiding the dead onto a good path in the Underworld and involved with royal conquest in this life, going before the pharaoh to open the way for him. Christie's Images

The Nomes — Cities and Gods

UPPER EGYPT

No	Location	Name	Main Towns	Deities
1	First Cataract to Geb-el-Silsila	Ta-Sety	Elephantine, Kom Ombo	Isis, Khnum, Sobek, Satis ,Anukis
2	Edfu area	Throne of Horus	Edfu	Horus
3	Hierakonopolis to North Esna	Shrine	Hierakonopolis, Latopolis	Horus, Nekhbet, Khnum, Neith
4	Armant and the Theban area	Sceptre	Thebes	Montu, Amun, Mut, Khonsu
5	Koptos	Two Falcons	Koptos, Qift	Min, Set
6	East to West bend of the Nile	Crocodile	Tentyris, Qena	Hathor
7	The Nile around Nag Hammadi	Sistrum	Diospolis-Parva	Bat
8	Abydos area	Great Land	Abydos	Osiris, Anuris
9	Akhmin area	Min	Panopolis	Min
10	North of Qaw-el-Kebir	Cobra	Antaeopolis	Set
11	West bank around Deir Rifa	Set	Shutb	Set
12	East bank opposite Asyut	Viper Mount	Deir el Gebrawi	Anti
13	West bank around Asyut	Upper Sycamore and Viper	Lykopolis	Anubis, Wepawawet
14	Around Meir and el-Qusiya	Lower Sycamore and Viper	Cusae	Hathor
15	Ashmunein and Antinoopolis, including el-Amarna	Hare	Hermopolis, Antinoopolis	Thoth, the Ogdoad
16	Beni-Hasan to North of el-Minya	Oryx	Zawyet el-Amwat	Pakhet
17	Samalut	Jackal	Hardai	Anubis
18	From the east bank of the Nile inc el-Hiba, to opposite el-Lahun	Anti	Ankyrononpolis	Anti
19	West bank of the Nile, from el-Bahnasa to Biba	Two Sceptres	Oxyrhynchus	Set
20	West bank of the Nile around Beni-Suef	South Sycamore	Herakleopolis, Krokodilopolis	Heryshaf
21	West bank of the Nile around el-Wasta, Meidum	North Sycamore	Meidum	Khnum
22	From Atfih to Memphis	Knife	Aphroditopolis	Hathor

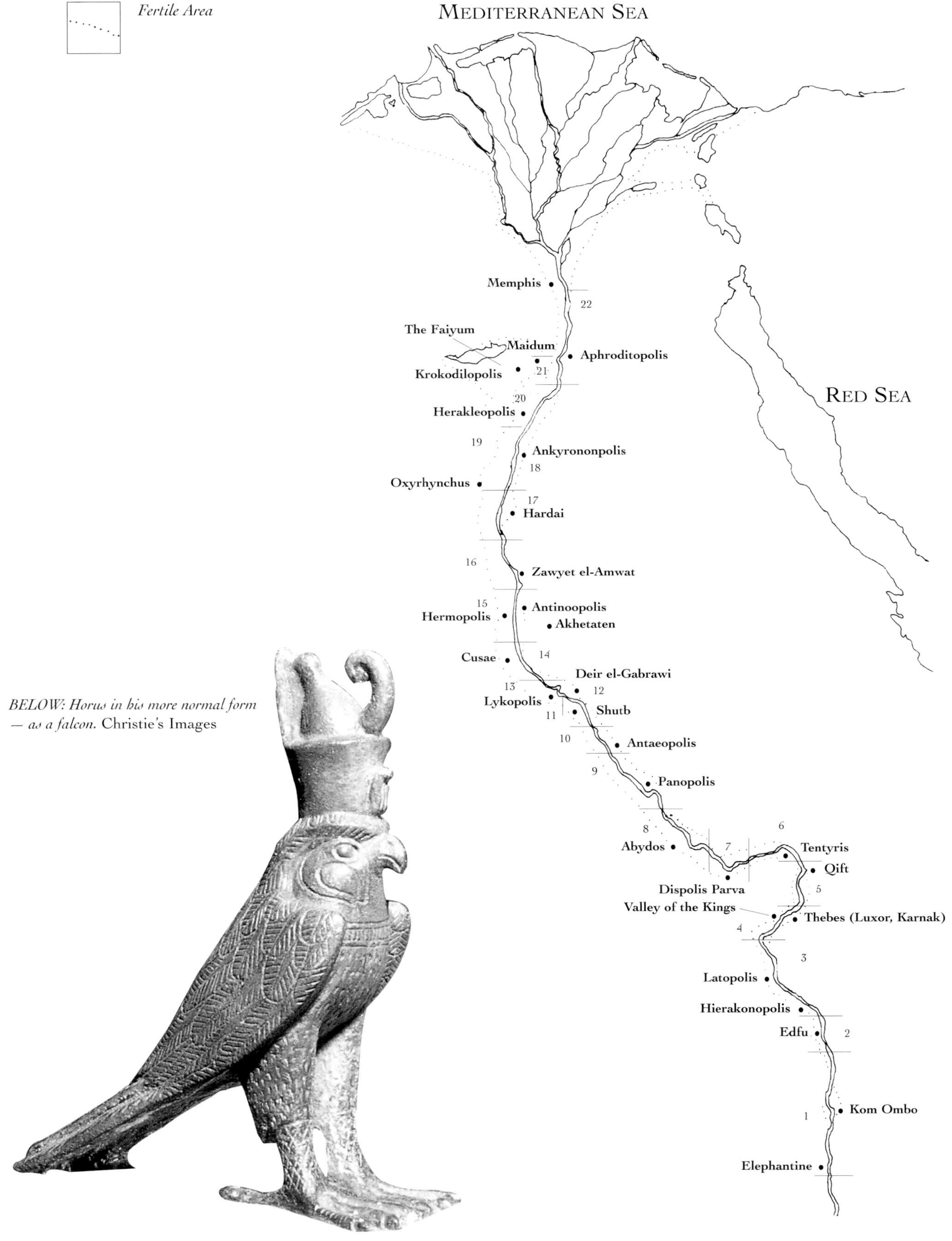

BELOW: Horus in his more normal form — as a falcon. Christie's Images

LOWER EGYPT

No	Location	Name	Main Towns	Deities
1	Memphis area	White Wall	Memphis	Ptah, Sokar, Apis
2	South-west delta	Foreleg	Letopolis	Horus, Kherty
3	North-west delta	West	Hermopolis Parva	Hathor
4	South-west delta	Southern Shield		Neith
5	Sais area to the coast	Northern Shield	Buto	Neith
6	Mid-delta to the coast	Mountain Bull	Xois	Re‘
7	North-west delta (along the Rosetta Nile Branch)	Western Harpoon		Ha
8	East delta	Eastern Harpoon	Pithom	Atum
9	Mid-delta to Busiris	Andjety	Busiris	Osiris, Andjety
10	South-east delta around Athribis	Black Ox	Athribis	Horus
11	Mid-east delta	Ox-count	Leontopolis	Shu,Tefnut
12	North-east delta	Calf and Cow	Sebennytos	Onuris
13	South-eastern apex of the delta.	Prospering Sceptre	Heliopolis	Atum
14	East-frontier coast	Foremost of the East	Pelusium	Set
15	North-eastern delta — the Damietta branch of the Nile	Ibis	Hermopolis	Thoth
16	North-eastern delta, Mendes to the coast	Fish	Mendes	Banbdjedet, Hatmehyt
17	North-east delta, the coast west of the Damietta Nile branch	Behdet	El-Balamun	Horus
18	North-east delta around Bubastis	Prince of the South	Bubastis	Bastet
19	North-east delta, inc Tanis	Prince of the North	Tanis	Wadjet
20	North-east delta, above Wadi Tummilat	Plumed Falcon of Sopedu	Saft el-Hinna	Sopedu

MEDITERRANEAN SEA

Hermopolis
el-Balamun
12
17
Alexandria
Buto
6
7
5
Xois
Hermopolis Parva
Sebennytos
Busiris
15
Mendes
16
19
Tanis
Pelusium
14
11
Leontopolis
20
Phakussa
9
3
18
Saft el-Hinna
Pithom
8
4
10
Bubastis
Athribis
Letopolis
2
Heliopolis
13
Giza
Memphis
1
Fertile Area

FAR LEFT: Seated statue of Zozer, a replica now sits where the original was found in a sealed chamber in the ruined temple at Saqqara. He built the first Egyptian pyramid around 2630BC. The damage to his eyes was caused by thieves gouging out the precious stones. Cairo Museum

LEFT: Hathor, the great sky-cow-mother goddess, second only to Isis in the pantheon, Hathor was the older and original mother of Horus.

OVERLEAF: The great pylon of the temple of Horus at Edfu. The temple was for centuries almost completely covered by buildings with only the gigantic sandstone pylons easily visible. Work to clear and restore the temple was started at the beginning of the 20th century. It is now the most complete temple in Egypt. Building started on the temple in 237BC and construction and decoration took until 57BC to finish — although the builders did take a 20-year break during the disturbances in Egypt under Ptolemy IV and V Epiphanes.

Archaeological Remains

UPPER EGYPT

Location	**Major Sites**
Philae	Greco-Roman centre of pilgrimage. Temples of Isis, Mandulis, Arensnuphis, Hathor
Elephantine and Aswan	Town, temples and rock-cut tombs spanning from Old to New Kingdoms. Nilometer.
Kom-Ombo	Greco-Roman Temple of Sobek and Haroeris.
Gebel el-Silsila	Sandstone quarries used in all periods. Rock-cut chapel of Harembab. Also rock-cut shrines of Kings and officials of the New Kingdom.
Edfu	Ptolemaic Temple of Horus. Tombs of Old and New Kingdoms. Pylon of Rameses III.
Kom el-Ahmar	Pre-dynastic settlements and cemeteries. Town and temple remains from all periods. Rock-cut tombs.
el-Kab	Temple of Nekhbet. Structures from all periods. Rock-cut tombs of 18th Dynasty.
Esna	Greco-Roman temple of Khnum. Cemeteries of the Middle Kingdom and later
el-Mo'alla	Rock-cut tombs of the 1st Intermediate Period.
Gebelein	Tombs of 1st Intermediate Period. Temple of Hathor — all periods.
Tod	Temple of Montu from the 5th Dynasty to the Greco-Roman Period.
Armant	Temple of Montu 11th Dynasty and later. Bull cemetery.
Thebes:	
Luxor	Temple of Amun.
Karnak	Precincts of Amun, Mut and Montu. Temple of Khons and others.
West Bank	Pharaonic mortuary temples. Temple of Amun. Ramesseum. Memnon Colossi. Temple of Hatshepsut. Rock-cut royal tombs — Valley of the Kings and Valley of the Queens. Private tombs from the 6th Dynasty onwards.
Nag' el-Madamud	Temple of Montu Greco-Roman period.
Naqada and Tukh	Pre-dynastic and early dynastic cemeteries. Mastaba tombs. Pyramid of Tukh.
Qus	Remains of the Temple of Haroeris and Heket. Cemeteries from early periods.
Qift	Remains of the Temple of Min from Middle Kingdom onwards.
Dendera	Temple of Hathor. Temple of Horus. Necropolis. Animal burials.
el-Qasr wa'l-Saiyad	Tombs from the 1st Intermediate Period.
Hiw	Two Greco-Roman temples. Cemeteries from all periods.
Abydos	Cemeteries from all periods. Royal tombs of the early dynasties. Temple of Osiris. Cenotaph. Temples of Seti I and Rameses II.
Beit Khallaf	Mastaba tombs of the 3rd Dynasty.
Ahkmin	Rock-cut chapels of Min (Thutmose III). Greco-Roman remains of a temple to Min.
Rock-cut tombs of various periods	
Wannina	Ptolemaic temples and tombs,
Qaw el-Kebir	Tombs from the 12th Dynasty.
Asyut	Tombs of the 1st Intermediate and Middle Kingdom periods.
Deir el-Gabrawi	Tombs of 6th Dynasty Nomarchs.
Meir	Tombs of 6th Dynasty Nomarchs, and 12th Dynasty.
el-Amarna	Remains of Akhenaten's brief capital. Rock-cut tombs of officials and Royal Tomb.
el-Sheik Sa'id	Tombs of 6th Dynasty Nomarchs.
Deir el-Bersha	Rock tombs of 12th Dynasty Nomarchs.
el-Ashmunein	Temples of Thoth 12th and Ramessid Dynasties.
Tuna el-Gebel	Stelae of Akhenaten. Animal catacombs. Greco-Egyptian Necropolis.
el-Sheik 'Ibada	Site of Antinoopolis. Temple of Rameses II.
Beni Hasan	Rock-cut tombs of 11th and 12th Dynasty Nomarchs. Rock-hewn Temple of Pakhet.

RIGHT: The Great Temple of Amun at Karnak was constructed over two millenia and was one of the most important sites in ancient Egypt. Massively endowed by the pharoahs, it covers nearly one square mile in area. Inside the fore or first court, near the second pylon, is a gigantic — 15m high — statue of Rameses II. Standing between the pharaoh's feet is his daughter Benta'anta. It was the main place of worship of the Theban triad — Amun, Mut and Khons.

OVERLEAF: The Colossi of Memnon. Named thus by visitors in Greek and Roman times, these two huge sandstone statues on the road from the Nile to Medinet Habu are in fact of Amenhotep III. The 18m (59ft) statues used to flank the entrance to his mortuary temple but are all that remain of the once vast complex. On either side of the pharaoh are his mother, Mutemwia, and his wife Tiye. The statues were severely damaged by the earthquake of 27BC — and one used to make a keening noise in the wind. This used to attract large numbers of tourists (some of their graffiti can still be seen) until restored by Roman Emperor Septimus Severus.

Location	Major Sites
Zawyet el-Amwat	Step Pyramid. Rock tombs of late Old Kingdom.
Tihna el-Gebel	Rock-cut tombs of the Old Kingdom. Greco-Roman temple remains and Necropolis.
el-Bahnasa	Site of Oxyrhynchus.
el-Hiba	Temple of Shoshenq I.
Dishasha	Late Old Kingdom tombs.
Ihnasya el-Medina	Temple of Harsaphus of 12th Dynasty. Tombs from the 1st Intermediate and various other periods.Temple of Rameses II.
Kom Medinet Ghurab	Temple of Thutmose III. Palace of Amenhotep III. Cemeteries.
el-Lahun	Pyramid complex of Senwosret II. Mastabas and graves of all periods.
The Faiyum	Temples and settlements, mainly Greco-Roman. Pylons at Hawara.
Maidum	First true pyramid (Huni-Snofru). Early 4th Dynasty Mastabas. Pyramid of Amenemhet I. Pyramid of Senwosret I.
LOWER EGYPT	
Memphis:	
Mit Rahina	Temple of Ptah. Colossi of Rameses II and a Sphinx. Numerous smaller temples from various periods. Embalming house for Apis bulls. Palace of Merneptah.
Dahshur	Pyramids of the 4th-12th and 13th Dynasties, including the Bent Pyramid.
Saqqara	First great stone monument, the great Imhotep's step pyramid built for Zozer. Remains of royal tombs of the 2nd Dynasty. Pyramids of 3rd-13th Dynasties. Private tombs from all periods. Serapeum and animal necropolis. Late Greco-Roman temples.
Abusir	Sun-Temple of Userkaf. Four pyramids of the 5th Dynasty. Private tombs from various periods.
Abu Ghurab	Sun-Temple of Neuserre. Two unfinished pyramids from the 3rd and 4th Dynasties.
Giza	The Pyramids of Khufu, Khepren and Menkaure. Private tombs, mainly from the Old Kingdom. The Great Sphinx. New Kingdom Temple of Harmakhis.
Abu Rawash	Pyramid of Ra'djedef. Cemeteries from the early dynasties, to the Old Kingdom and the Greco-Roman Period.
Ausim	Scattered Late Period monuments.
Kom Abu Billo	Ptolemaic Temple of Hathor. Necropolis used from the 6th Dynasty onwards.
Kom el-Hisn	Temple of Sakhmet-Hathor of the Middle Kingdom. Cemeteries of the Middle and New Kingdoms.
Naukratis	Greek trading town. Greek temples but also Temples of Amun and Thoth.
Alexandria	Ptolemaic and Roman Temple of Serapis. Catacombs. Classical remains.
Abusir	Unfinished Ptolemaic temple. Animal necropolis.
Sa el-Hagar	Remains of the Temple of Neith.
Behbeit el-Hagar	Temple of Isis in late and Ptolemaic periods.
Tell Atrib	Temple of Amasis. Town, temple and necropolis of Greco-Roman period.
Tell el-Muqdam	Remains of the Temple of Mihos. Tomb of Queen Kamama.
Samannud	Temple remains of Onuris-Shu, late and Greco-Roman periods.
el-Baqliya	Town and Temple of Thoth. Necropolis with Ibis cemetery.
Tell el-Rub'a	Late Old Kingdom Mastabas. Temple of Amasis. Ram cemetery.
Heliopolis	Temple of Re' and surrounding precincts and structures from all periods. Obelisk of Senwosret I. Tombs of the High-Priests of Heliopolis of the 6th Dynasty and later. Ramessid tombs of Mnevis Bulls.
Tell el-Yahudiya (Leontopolis)	Temple of Rameses II. Remains of town called Onias. Cemeteries of the Middle Kingdom and later.
Tell Basta (Bubastis)	Temple of Bastet. Smaller temples of various dynasties. Cat cemeteries.
Saft el-Hinna	Temple of Sopedu.
el-Khata'na and Qantir	Town and temple remains from Middle Kingdom period. Palace remains from 2nd Intermediate Period. Temple of Set. Remains of a colossus of Rameses II.

ABOVE: Avenue of Sphinxes leading to the Temple of Luxor. The avenue was commissioned by Nectenebo I to flank the processional route which connected the temples of Luxor and Karnak used in particular for the annual Opet Festival. This photograph shows the first pylon — famous for its reliefs showing the battle of Kadesh between Egyptians and Hittites — with, in front of it, two seated and one standing figure. There were three other figures and a pair to the single obelisk still visible: they were given to France in the 19th century and the obelisk is today in the Place de la Concorde in Paris.

LEFT: The Mortuary Temple of Rameses III at Medinet Habu is closely modelled on the Ramesseum. The complex includes a small palace in which the pharaoh would stay during festivals; after his death this became the symbolic residence for his spirit. Inside the First Court there is a row of collossi of the pharaoh.

Location	Major Sites
Tell Nabasha	Ramessid Temple of Wadjit. Temple by Amasis. Greco-Roman town remains. Late Period cemetery.
San el-Hagar (Tanis)	Temple of Amun and various other buildings. Precinct of Mut. Royal Tombs of 21st and 22nd Dynasties.
Tell el-Maskhuta	Temple enclosure.
THE OASES	
el-Kharga:	
Ain-Amur	Roman period settlement and temple.
Hibis	Temple of Amun.
Qasr el-Ghueida	Temple of Amun, Mut and Khons of 25th Dynasty.
Nadura	Roman period temple.
Qasr-Zaiyan	Ptolemaic and Roman temple.
Qasr-Dush	Roman temple of Serapis and Isis.
el-Dakhla:	
Balat	Mastabas of the 6th Dynasty and first Intermediate Period. New Kingdom Temple of Mut. Tombs of the 3rd Intermediate and Roman periods.
Amhada	1st Intermediate Period tombs.
Mut	Destroyed temple and objects of the 3rd Intermediate Period.
el-Qasr	Temple of Thoth from Greco-Roman period. Necropolis.
Deil el-Hagar	Temple of first century AD.
Qaret el-Muzawwaqa	Tombs of the Roman period.
el-Smant el Kharab	Roman town site, with ruined temple.
Bahariya:	
el-Qasr and el-Bawiti	Tomb of Amenhotpe Huy-18th-19th Dynasty. Chapels and tombs from the reigns of Apries, Amasis and the Greco-Roman period. Temple of Alexander the Great. Destroyed triumphal arch of the Roman period.
el-Hayz	Small Roman period centre.
Siwa:	
Aghurmi	Temple of 26th Dynasty and Ptolemaic Period. (Presumed to be where Alexander the Great consulted the oracle of Jupiter-Ammon.)
Umm el Ebeida	Temple of Nectenebo II.
Gebel el-Mawta	Cemeteries and a few smaller temples. Necropolis of the 26th Dynasty and the Greco-Roman Period.
NUBIA	
Dabod	Temple of Amun.
Tafa	Remains of two Roman temples.
Beit el-Wali	Temple of Amun-Re', built by Rameses II.
Kalabsha	Temple of Mandulis, Isis and Osiris built by Augustus Caesar. Late Ptolemaic Period gate.
Dendur	Temple of Peteese and Pihor.
Gerf Hussein	Rock-cut temple of Rameses II.
el-Dakka	Greco-Roman temple.
Quban	12th Dynasty fort.
'Amada	Temple of Amun-Re' and Re'-Harakhty, built by Thutmose III and Amenhotep II.
el-Subu'a	Temple of Horus. Temple of Rameses II.
el-Derr	Rock-cut temple, built by Rameses II.
el-Lessiya	Rock-cut chapel of Thutmose III.
Qasr Ibrim	New Kingdom fort. Remains of Temple of Taharqa. Rock-cut shrines of the Viceroys of Kush of the 18th and 19th Dynasties.

RIGHT: The Ramesseum at Karnak is dedicated to Amun-United-with-Eternity and Rameses II whose mortuary temple it is. The Greeks called it the Tomb of Osymandyas, which in turn inspired Shelley, on seeing an engraving of the great fallen statue of Rameses II, to write his famous poem Ozymandius. The fallen colossus is just visible on the right of this photograph which shows well the headless Osiride statues of Rameses II.

Location	**Major Sites**
Aniba	Middle-Kingdom fort. Temple of Horus of 18th Dynasty. Cemeteries of various periods.
Abu Simbel	Two temples of Rameses II. Great Temple with rock-hewn facade, with four colossi of Rameses II seated. Small Temple of Hathor, with colossi of Queen Nefertari.
Abahuda	Rock-cut Temple of Amun-Re' and Thoth, built by Haremhab.
Gebel el-Shams	Rock-cut chapel of Paser — a viceroy of Kush. Cemeteries.
Qustul	New Kingdom cemeteries and of other periods.
Faras	Remains of Temple of Tutankhamun. Rock-cut chapel of Hathor.
Aksha	Temple and chapels of Seti I and Rameses II.
Dibeira	Rock-cut tombs of various periods,
Buhen	Middle Kingdom fort and Temple of Isis and Min and Temple of Horus.
Kor	Fort of Middle and New Kingdoms.
Mirgissa	Fort, town and cemeteries, mainly of Middle Kingdom. Small New Kingdom sanctuary of Hathor.
Kumma	Middle Kingdom fort. Temple of Khnum, built by Thutmose II and III.
Semna	Middle Kingdom fort. Temples of Thutmose III, and Taharqa.
'Amara	Remains of a town of the 19th Dynasty, with a temple of Rameses II.
Sedeinga	Temple of Amenhotep III. Cemeteries.
Gebel Dosha	Rock-cut chapel of Tuthmosis III.
Soleb	Temple of Amenhotep III. New Kingdom cemetery.
Sesebi	Remains of New Kingdom town, with Temples of Aten and the Theban Triad, built by Akhenaten and Seti I.
Kawa	Temples of Amun, various periods.
el-Kurru	Pyramids of 25th Dynasty pharaohs.
Sanam	Temple of Amun-Re', built by Taharqa. Palace complex and cemeteries of the 25th Dynasty.
Gebel Barkal	Meriotic pyramids. Temples and chapels to Amun-Re', built in various periods,
Nuri	Remains of pyramids of Taharqa and others.
Meroe	Remains of temples and pyramids of the Meroitic Period.
Ba'sa	Meroitic temple remains.
Naqa	Remains of Meroitic temples.

ABOVE: Kalabsha temple on Lake Nasser near Aswan is dedicated to the Nubian god Mandulis, as well as Osiris and Isis, and was built during the reign of Augustus Caesar. Since the beginning of the 20th century the temple had spent much of each year under water, so in 1962-63 it was dismantled and moved to New Kalabsha, near the Aswan Dam.

LEFT: The Nile and modern town of Aswan. To this day an important town in Egypt, consequently very few ancient buildings survive in the area.

ABOVE LEFT: The Temple of Isis on Philae island at Aswan. It was a late foundation by Egyptian standards, but it became in Roman times the premier pilgrimage destination for worshippers of the cult of Isis. The temple was also the last surviving functioning temple of the ancient Egyptian religion until dissolved by Emperor Justinian in AD551.

FAR LEFT: Temple of Khnum at Esna. Only the Roman hypostyle hall survives, the latest major religious building to have been found preserved.

ABOVE and RIGHT: The Mortuary Temple of Hatshepsut was used in later years as a Coptic monastery, the Deir el-Bahri, which has given the area its name. With the magnificent backdrop of the Theban cliffs behind, it is the remarkable work of the queen's architect Senmut, rising in a series of terraces up to the sanctuary of Amun. Hatshepsut ruled Egypt following the death of her husband, Thutmose II, and was succeeded by her son, Thutmose III. Unimpressed by his long wait for the throne, he subsequently defaced many of her images.

ABOVE: Saqqara had as many as 15 pyramids — although some of them are barely distinguishable mounds today. Perhaps best known is the step pyramid the royal architect Imhotep built for Zozer (Djoser). Imhotep was deified, one of the very few who weren't pharaohs to receive the honour.

LEFT: The Temple of Hathor is the principal building at Dendera and one of the best preserved in Egypt. It is dedicated to Horus the Elder and Hathor the goddess of love and beauty, although she is also associated here with Isis. The facade has six Hathor-headed columns. The temple had close links with that of Horus at Edfu; indeed, once a year the goddess journeyed to Edfu escorted by priests and cheering crowds to visit Horus who came out to meet her on his boat. The famous zodiac ceiling is now in the Louvre.

RIGHT: Splendid aerial view of the temples at Abu Simbel. Centre left is the Temple of Rameses II and to its right is the temple of Nefertari. This view gives a clear indication of the amount of work necessary to resite them when they were inundated by the construction of the Aswan dam. The entire sandstone temple was carefully cut into 1,050 blocks and reassembled 210m behind and above the newly-created Lake Nasser between 1964-68.

BELOW RIGHT: The entrance to Rameses II's temple at Abu Simbel dedicated to himself, the sun-god Re'-Herakhte and Amun. The four immense statues of the pharaoh dwarf smaller figures around his knees — his wives and daughters — and the image of Ra'-Herakhte above the doorway.

FAR RIGHT: Detail of one of the 65ft statues of Rameses II on the front entrance of his temple. This too moved above the newly-created Lake Nasser.

BELOW FAR RIGHT: Temple of Queen Nefertari and Hathor at Abu Simbel. In the centre is Queen Nefertari (see detail BELOW) with her two daughters, princesses Merytamun and Hentawi. Flanking her on either side is Rameses II with her four sons, princes Meryatum, Meryre, Amunhirkhopshef and Rahrirwemenef.